MW00331257

Margaret -
May this book
validate for ya the power
of love -
and bring ya comfort,
peace and hope.
Blessings -
Susan Apollox

Praise for Susan Barbara Apollon, *Touched by the Extraordinary* and *Healing Stories of Love, Loss, and Hope* . . .

"*Healing Stories of Love, Loss, and Hope* is food for the soul—I simply couldn't put it down."

> — CHRISTIANE NORTHRUP, MD
> Ob/Gyn Physician and Author of the *New York Times* best sellers: *Women's Bodies, Women's Wisdom* and *The Wisdom of Menopause*

"Inspired and inspiring. *Healing Stories of Love, Loss, and Hope* by psychologist and grief counselor Susan Apollon is highly recommended reading, especially for those who could benefit by the comforting example of others who have had to deal with life's inevitable tribulations."

> — JAMES A. COX
> Editor, *Midwest Book Review*

"This is a book that you will never put away as it will lift your spirit and soul on a daily basis."

> — BETH BAUGHMAN DuPREE, MD, FACs
> Breast Surgeon and Author, *The Healing Consciousness: A Doctor's Journey to Healing*

"This is a beautiful book filled with compassion and understanding, compiled by a very loving and wise old soul. I highly recommend it."

> — YANNI MANIATES
> Author *Magical Keys to Self-Mastery* and Co-Author of *Intuition is Easy and Fun*

"*Touched by the Extraordinary Book Two*! What a gift! What a treasure! . . . .All those true stories of life and the after-life . . . serve to bring us hope and remind us that 'Life is Forever!' Thank you, Susan. We your readers, appreciate you."

> — JOHN HARRICHARAN
> Author and International Speaker

"Reading the words of others reinforced my belief that those who have passed, so fiercely loved, are with us always. Your twelve suggestions for healing are wonderful! . . . Your words about grief and grieving touched me deeply as I am reminded of my sense of loss and grieving for the slow disappearance of my mother over the years from her Parkinson's. Thank you for the permission to feel this; it is truly comforting!"

— BERYL KATZ
Founder of S.A.G.E. (Senior Adults for Greater Education)

"Having a guide to show us how death fits into life, how not to just survive but flourish in these desperate times is so important. Susan is the consummate guide. You can feel Susan's warmth literally radiating from these pages."

— ERIC LEVIN, PH.D.
Clinical Psychologist in Private Practice, Clinical Assistant Professor, Dept of Psychology, Drexel University

"I wish I had known Susan when my father passed away. Though it has been fifteen years since his death, reading her book has been very therapeutic for me in dealing with my loss . . . *Touched by the Extraordinary* is filled with stories that can assist in the healing process . . . It will provide peace and hope for so many."

— JEFFREY HERMAN, DO
Psychiatrist

"Susan Apollon's new book lovingly carries her readers from stories of unbearable loss to the gateway of hope and personal renewal. Insightful and compassionate Apollon helps share the journey of life to death and to answered prayers. A tender and helpful contribution to all concerned with spiritual healing."

— LANCE J. SUSSMAN, PH.D.
Senior Rabbi, Reform Congregation Keneseth Israel, Elkins Park, PA, Visiting Professor, Dept of Religion, Princeton University

"These stories are not only a balm for the soul and heart but a real-life-endorsement of the power of Love, healing and hope . . . everyone in some way can benefit from this wisdom."

— JILL SAMO, PH.D.
Clinical Psychologist

"The true nature of the mind is Luminescence and Love. *Touched by the Extraordinary Book Two* shows us how Divine Consciousness manifests in our lives, always knowing we are Love."

— SANDRA ESNER
Founder of *Angels Without Wings*

"*Touched by the Extraordinary Book Two* is beautiful, moving and will provide much needed guidance to those dealing with grief after loss of a loved one. Susan has given us yet another spiritual gift to share with our patients to help them in their healing journey."

— AMY HARVEY, MD
Physician of Obstetrics and Gynecology

"In her inimitable style, and through her pure expression of Love, Susan sees us through the eyes of an angel, sharing with us stories to help us through our journey of Life. Her stories aid and support us through the difficult passage we face in our dealings with Life's Challenges."

— ROBERT SASSON, MD
Pediatrician and Author, *Visions of Thought*

"These pages are sacred. Within them you will discover that we are never alone and that there is a Divine Purpose in our being here. There is an eternal quality to Susan's lessons . . . Keep it in a safe place and read from it often . . . a gentle reminder that the peace found in the moment, and healing, is but a thought away."

— WILLIAM E. HABLITZEL, MD
Author of *Dying Was the Best Thing That Ever Happened to Me*

"In *Touched by the Extraordinary Book Two*, Susan Apollon' poignant, powerful stories about loss and hope help us to remember we are connected to something beyond ourselves—something unseen but real, something transcendent and true, s spiritual cord that ties us to that Divine Source and to each other."

— RABBI ELLIOT STROM
Rabbi, Congregation Shir Ami, Newtown, PA

"These accounts of love, loss, and hope prove that, although life breaks many of us, we can grow stronger at the break. Love and our connection with a transcendent power have healing effects that we often underestimate, as these inspirational stories show."

— LARRY DOSSEY, MD
Author of *The Power of Premonition*

"If you have ever suffered the intense, hollow pain of loss or grief, or experienced the yearning to feel the presence of your departed, this collection of first-hand stories is a comforting balm for your soul."

— ANITA BERGEN
Author, *Life and Other Options*

"Susan guides us with the compassion and healing we all need, and are called upon to offer to others. Her sense of God's presence and purpose for each of us, and her respect for others and their spirituality are the strength of her hope and healing."

— FR. LARRY SNYDER
Episcopal Priest

Touched by the Extraordinary

BOOK TWO

Healing Stories of Love, Loss & Hope

TOUCHED
by the
EXTRAORDINARY
BOOK TWO

HEALING STORIES OF
LOVE, LOSS & HOPE

Susan Barbara Apollon

FOREWORD BY WILLIAM E. HABLITZEL, M.D.

MATTERS
OF THE
Soul

Yardley, Pennsylvania

Touched by the Extraordinary, Book Two:
Healing Stories of Love, Loss, and Hope

Matters of the Soul, LLC
Box 403
Yardley, PA 19067

ISBN: 978-0-9754036-9-3

Cover and Interior design by Desktop Miracles, Inc.

Publisher's Cataloging-In-Publication Data
(Prepared by The Donohue Group, Inc.)

Apollon, Susan Barbara.
    Touched by the extraordinary. Book two, Healing stories of love, loss & hope / Susan Barbara Apollon ; foreword by William Hablitzel.
        p. ; cm.
    Portion of title: Healing stories of love, loss & hope
    ISBN: 978-0-9754036-9-3
    1. Loss (Psychology) 2. Life change events—Psychological aspects. 3. Future life. 4. Bereavement—Psychological aspects. I. Hablitzel, William E. II. Title.
III. Title: Healing stories of love, loss & hope
BF575.D35 A66   2010
155/.93   2010905952

Printed in the United States of America

For Warren

You are my North Star, my Sun, and my Moon.
Your love supports, replenishes,
comforts, and embraces me,
while feeding my soul and enabling
me to be available to others.
May our journey together be
blessed throughout eternity.

Table of Contents

Acknowledgements

With Appreciation and Gratitude

Writing this book has been an experience of great love and dedication. This would not have come into being if it were not for the heartwarming support and kindness of those who have agreed to share their personal stories of healing so that others might also find gifts of healing in reading them.

My love and thanks to each of you, including Janie Hermann, Beth DuPree, Kim Wencl, Sharon J., Terry Kovalchick, Natalie Kaye, Jennifer Brinton Robkin, Trish Myers, David Kane, Linda Marshall, Brenda Taylor, Valerie Hartman, Dan Stoughton, Jeff Werner, Shelly Greenwald, Diane, CoraLyn Hughes, LouLou Wolfson, Bonnie Frank Carter, Mira Borodovsky, Cheryl Baldi, Deron Nardo, Mary Ellen Winn, John

Harricharan, Mary Kane, Carol Magner, Charlotte Bishop, Michel Zeibari and Rosalie Schack.

To each of you who agreed to sit for an interview, or who took the time to send me your story, you have my heartfelt thanks and gratitude for your precious gift of time and energy. Your words are providing others with needed hope, optimism, and a perspective of positive expectations about surviving life's more difficult, challenging times. You are the heart of this book, and for this, I thank you so very, very much. By sharing your healing moments, you enable others to have theirs.

For a book to be successful, it requires a superb editor. I am deeply grateful to you, Cheryl Baldi, for your magical gift of weaving the words I have written into a fabric of warmth and beauty that touches the heart and delights the soul. For the long hours you have worked, your deep and pure dedication to bringing these stories to the reader, and for wanting to maintain their genuine essence, I thank you from my heart. You have shared my vision, and for this I am extremely blessed.

A book is often remembered by its cover, among other things. My thanks to Barry and Del and all the crew at Desktop Miracles Publishing for dressing up *Touched by the Extraordinary* in the most perfect fashion, along with creating the most beautiful, artistic cover. Your work is impeccable! Additionally, I have appreciated your never-ending support, readiness to answer any and all of my questions, as well as your amazing, creative energy and productivity.

The process of writing a book is often lonely and sometime stressful. I am so grateful for the loving support of my family and dear friends. It feels wonderful to know that you have been there for me with your compassion, love, understanding, and caring (especially when I have had to turn down precious invitations to spend time with you). This has meant much more to me than I can adequately convey. Thank you all so very much.

John Harricharan, my sincere thanks to you for your gentle nudges for me to bring forth this book, one that would be filled with beautiful stories of those dealing with various kinds of grief. Knowing how close you were to Elisabeth Kubler-Ross, and always treasuring my short time with her, I often feel her in my midst as a quiet and supportive Presence.

Bill Hablitzel, knowing how extremely busy you are with your teaching of clinical medicine at the University of Cincinnati College of Medicine, your work as an internist in the rural areas of Ohio, and your own writing, I am extremely grateful that you agreed to take the time to write the Foreword for this book. Only a few people recognize the healing power of story as well as you do. The powerful stories you have so exquisitely written in *Dying Was the Best Thing That Ever Happened to Me* are filled with truth and wisdom for healing the body, mind and soul.

And finally, my heartfelt thanks to you, Warren. You have so patiently been supporting me with your quiet understanding and love. You tenderly watch over me, as well as ground me. Knowing you are here gives me the energy and ability to keep going, even when I am tired and weary. Thank you, my love, for all you are and all you do.

Foreword

by William E. Hablitzel, M.D.

When I saw that the package sitting against my door late one evening was from Yardley, Pennsylvania, I knew what was inside. I had been expecting the manuscript of Susan Apollon's new book for a number of weeks and it couldn't have arrived at a worse time. It had been a horrendous week—office schedules choked with problems that seemingly had no solutions, days that started deep in darkness and ended much the same, and endless hours spent drifting amidst the pain and suffering of my patients—and I wondered if the needs of others had exceeded my capacity to give.

The most amazing thing happened when I opened that package and started to read in the early morning hours of what had already become the next day. As I shared the journey of Kim and David—parents who each lost a child to fire only to discover that flames could not consume the love and hope that their children left behind—the fatigue that haunted me for days simply faded away. In the images painted by Luca the dog and Grace Boy the swan, I could see the face of the old lady that I helped to smile just the day before.

Dawn was breaking across the Appalachian hills that I call home when I read the astonishing tale of Malika and how through the miracle of intuition her father's love made her life possible. My attention was drawn to the study window through which I watched a morning's incredible beauty unfold. The day's first light seeped through the woods and set the hillsides aglow in autumn splendor. A white-tailed deer foraged nearby, dew still clinging to his antlers. A tufted titmouse extracted a carefully selected sunflower seed from the feeder hanging a short distance away. The beauty was stunning and brought moistness to my eyes. It was beauty that somehow I could not see just hours before.

Such is the power of story. It can heal.

There are moments in life powerful enough to change us instantly and forever. Far too often, though, these special moments come when we are not present to notice, lost in the dramas of yesterday or our plans for tomorrow. Imagine knowing that such a moment is close at hand. You will find it within the pages of this remarkable book.

We live complicated lives in a confusing world filled with disasters of unprecedented scale, mass media that bathes us in a continuous shower of fear and worry, and hectic days filled with too much to do and too little time to do it. It is in these special moments, however, when confusion can clear to understanding, fear can melt away to peace, and scarcity can turn into abundance. They are moments that can be found in the lives that surround us.

There is great wisdom in those lives. It is wisdom that offers us hope when we are adrift in the void that we feel through loss. It is wisdom that helps us recognize meaning in the seeming randomness of our lives. It is wisdom that helps us discover that our potential is without limits. It is wisdom that can be ours through their stories.

Psychologists know how to listen, but Susan is not your ordinary psychologist. She is very special. When she listens, she hears the story, sees the lesson that can help shape life, and shares the wonders that she finds there with others. We do not have to become ill, face tragedy, develop cancer, or even encounter death to learn the incredible lessons that can be found in such human experiences—we can learn from those who have been there.

The pages that follow are sacred. Within them you will discover that we are never alone and that there is a Divine purpose in our being here. There is an eternal quality to Susan's lessons and they will wait patiently within the stories of this wonderful book until your soul hungers to understand more about Love, Loss, and Hope. Keep it in a safe place and read from it often. It will help guide your journey to wonders beyond comprehension. Sometimes even our most treasured truths fade from our awareness when the treadmill of our lives runs particularly fast. Susan's book can do for you what it has done for me; a gentle reminder that the peace found in the present moment and healing, are but a thought away.

Medical school taught me all about cure and residency helped perfect skills that could make curing possible, but it wasn't enough. When I started my practice I realized that I knew nothing about healing and that there was a profound difference between it and curing. Special teachers—my patients—would help me come to understand through their incredible stories and special souls that they have shared part of their journey with me.

In the words, wisdom, and love of Susan Barbara Apollon I have been, as you most surely will be, *Touched by the Extraordinary.*

WILLIAM E. HABLITZEL, MD
Author of *Dying Was the Best Thing That Ever Happened to Me* and *It Was Only a Moment Ago*

Introduction

*Here is a test to find whether your
mission on earth is finished:
If you're alive, it isn't.*

Richard Bach,
Illusions: The Adventures of a Reluctant Messiah

Because you have chosen to read this book, no matter how old you are, I know in my heart that you have experienced the loss of someone or something you dearly loved. Within the following pages, it is my hope that you will find a connection with one or more of the stories my patients and others have shared. I offer these stories because they demonstrate that love and loss are a part of life; in fact, they are a necessary part of life.

Many years ago, Judith Viorst wrote a book, *Necessary Losses*, a perfect title, I think, given that we have little choice or control over the losses we experience. But experiencing loss also enables us to live out the potential of our soul.

Consider your own loss or losses, not only the pain you experienced by the separation from what and whom you loved, but the lessons you learned by having to journey through grief. Love and loss are necessary, because they become our teachers, instructing us how to live our lives with greater wisdom and joy. With each loss we sustain, we are given the opportunity to change, grow, and learn.

You may wonder, in mourning your loved one, why it is essential to grieve and endure such profound suffering.

Simply, it is because you choose to love. If you did not live lovingly and love deeply, you would not feel the pain of separation. But neither would you feel the joy, passion, and happiness that living fully and loving deeply bring.

To live means to feel the pain of separation from those to whom you are attached and from whom you derive a sense of purpose and a reason to live.

We think of loss as physical death and separation from a deceased loved one. But we also grieve when we are separated from our expectations, our dreams, and a future that we imagined. When parents lose a child, they not only grieve the loss of that child and the child's future, but their own future as well. Their futures are robbed of watching their child grow, sharing with that child the celebrations and joy that birthdays, graduations, and grandchildren bring.

Loss takes other forms. When a loved one, a friend, or even a business associate abandons us or betrays our trust, we experience loss, and we grieve. If our dreams of pursuing a specific career, such as becoming a teacher or a lawyer, an actor or a dentist, are not realized, we suffer profound disappointment, frustration, fear—in other words, we experience loss, and in our suffering, grieve.

Other difficulties arise in our lives. A young adult child announces he or she is gay, and we grieve for the traditional future we assumed we would have with that child. If we dream of being a parent or a grandparent, and life does not support this dream, we grieve. If our belief system is attached to and represented by a well known politician, philosopher, author, or athlete who dies, we feel a sense of loss for that person who, physically, has left us. When others we love or admire fall on difficult times, we also share their pain. This, simply, is the way it is, if we are caring and compassionate human beings.

The question is: how do we go on? How do we help ourselves? How do we help others? The answer lies in hope and love. Love is who we are, love of self and love for All There Is. Loss is part of our journey, and hope is what sustains us.

What is hope? Like love, it is hard to define, but easy to recognize, a state of being that compels us to go on. It is a feeling that we have what we need to continue our journey to the next moment. It is remembering that the sun will come up in the morning, regardless of how we feel the evening before. It is a fullness that fills every cell in our hearts, urging us forward, as we break into a smile and say, "Yes, I hear you. Let's get moving! We have a life to live, things to do, places to go, and more love to experience!"

We all need hope. As souls, we journey in physical bodies, traversing a life that is dually lived. We experience safety through attachment to the physical world, but we also are comforted and cared for by a trust in the non-physical, spiritual part of our reality. Two different roads, available for us and from which we choose, moment by moment.

Life provides us with a myriad of opportunities to choose hope. Any life-changing experience—a divorce, loss of a job, placing a loved one with Alzheimer's in a facility—causes pain and grief, but we are better able to sustain the loss when we find someone or something to offer us hope.

Hope has many voices. Often hope is found simply in the loving call from a neighbor, a friend, or family member who says, "I am here for you as long as you need for me to be here, and even then I will still be here for you."

If you have lost a part of your body—a breast, a part of your lung, your hearing, your sight—hope materializes when a sense of normalcy is restored and you realize that, in spite of your loss, you will be able to continue to experience a good quality of life.

Hope comes in the form of synchronicities. When one event occurs and is followed by another, which is in complete alignment with the first, we sense we are not alone. We know, intuitively throughout our beings, that what we are experiencing is the universe lovingly embracing us. We feel as though we are being watched over, and that our angels may really be hearing us as we speak with them, mind to mind.

One such synchronicity recently came to my attention. According to Shelly, on Mother's Day a few years ago, she experienced a lovely connection with her son, Adam. He had died several years earlier, and Shelly still missed him deeply. Although she would have loved a slice of her favorite dessert, peanut butter pie, she did not really feel like going out, but when friends called to invite her and her husband to dinner at the Cheesecake Factory she decided, reluctantly, to go.

Much to Shelley surprise, when she walked into the restaurant, she immediately spotted the refrigerated case in which there was a delicious looking pie. On the sign it read, "Adam's Peanut Butter Pie!" Need we say more?

I feel compelled to share several incidents that occurred during these past few days—all of which sustain my hope that I am one with All There Is—that we, as souls, do not die, and that we are available, always, for our loved ones, even as they transition. An awareness that I am being guided ever so lovingly by those who have left physically brings me immeasurable comfort.

At dinner several days ago, my husband received a call from a patient telling him that a very dear friend of ours, Theresa, had suffered a stroke earlier that day. She was in the hospital and was not expected to live beyond the weekend. Immediately, we went to the hospital where we found Theresa, conscious and aware of our presence, and despite the pain she was experiencing, cognizant of what we were saying.

Theresa and her husband, Lou, who had died four years earlier, were two of our oldest, closest friends, very much like family. While Theresa lay in her hospital bed, I sat next to her, energetically sharing with her Reiki and other energy modalities, hoping to soothe and comfort her. Her nephew, Deron, told me that she had asked for me that morning. Oddly, during the past week, I had written several notes to remind myself to call Theresa. I felt bad that we hadn't spoken in awhile, and I wanted to see her.

Clearly, we were connecting with one another, mind to mind. What is interesting is that Theresa could not identify the woman who called my husband to tell us of her stroke. And we still do not know how she knew to call us. But, it was a gift, and I was so grateful! Knowing that we are part of a greater consciousness, or Oneness, I also wondered if the call came through Lou, or her angels.

That evening, and the next, my husband and I were able to be with Theresa and Deron. The rest of the family arrived on Saturday night, just before one o'clock in the morning. It was that evening that I experienced another moment of incredible hopefulness.

I was seated next to Theresa, gently sending her warm, peaceful energy, when Deron leaned over to kiss his beloved aunt and to tell her that her family would be arriving soon. As I leaned to the left, to make room for Deron, I looked up and was stunned to see Lou in Deron's face. Lou had been a second father to Deron. The image lasted just a second, but however briefly, I saw Lou, and it was amazing.

While we sat with Theresa and Deron, in my heart, I felt Lou's presence. I know, based on many years of research, that in the final hours, our loved ones are present for us. They bring their warmth, love, and comfort to us as we prepare to leave our physical bodies. Seeing Lou in Deron's face validated this for me. As Deron leaned over to kiss his aunt, Lou's energetic presence emerged to provide support and love to his beloved wife.

Theresa died the following day, after saying "I love you" and "goodbye" to her nephews and family. We all were grateful that she no longer had to suffer and that she, finally, was free to be with Lou and her loved ones once again. Being able to feel and see Lou's presence was a gift of hope for all of us as Theresa was transitioning.

Hope also comes to us through prayer. When we pray and our prayers are answered, we are comforted and become more hopeful.

One of my dear friends, Tom, is exceptionally spiritual. He prays daily and often asks for a sign that he is being heard. Each time his request is answered, his hope increases; he feels more confident that his needs will be met, and that he is not alone. During his evening prayers, he once asked for roses as a sign that his prayers were being heard. The following day, one of his customers, unexpectedly, arrived at Tom's place of work with a bouquet of roses. Over the years, he, frequently, has requested roses, and always, has received them within twenty-four hours.

I, too, while praying, once asked that I be given roses as a sign that my prayers were being heard. The following day, I was astonished as I entered my waiting room to find rose petals scattered on the floor—everywhere! They also were scattered over the floor in my private office, and on my desk was a beautiful bouquet of my favorite, star-gazer lilies. My patient, Terry, an intuitive and spiritual soul, had brought them to me, but she also recognized that she had served as a messenger for Divine energy.

Finally, hope comes to us through messages from our deceased loved ones, whether it is a family member, a friend, or a pet. Often, when we are feeling great pain and thinking of our loved one, we experience a soft touch or cool breeze on our forehead, neck or back. It might be a feather that falls each time we fill with sadness. It might be the blinking of lights, or a television turning on as our heart aches with our loss. For some, our loved ones send ladybugs, butterflies or dragonflies, for others, a special bird, or a squirrel.

This book is my gift to you, in the hope that you will become more conscious of the ways in which we are interconnected energetically, in what I call Oneness. Our separation from one another is an illusion. Accepting this enables us to be transformed by the experiences we have throughout our lives.

Give yourself permission to see and feel the extraordinary events in your own life. In internalizing them, you also will find your perspective about life and its meaning will change, resulting in growth and expansion of your soul. You may even notice that you will be blessed with feeling more peace, confidence, security, and joy!

1

Losing a Child

God is closest to those with broken wings.

JEWISH SAYING

The Letter

Treasure the love you receive above all.
It will survive long after your gold
and good health have vanished.

Og Mandino

It was August 30th, and there it was on the front page of *USA Today*: the article about college, off-campus, fatal, house fires. My daughter, Liz, had died in an off-campus house fire three years earlier.

In early August, I received a phone call from a reporter working on the story. The reporter had done extensive, nationwide research on all fatal off-campus fires since 2000 and was interested in the circumstances of the fire in which Liz died. All too often these college fires are linked to smoking and drinking, and in fact, these behaviors were contributing factors in Liz's death. The editors of the paper wanted to run the story in time for those college students moving into off-campus housing for the upcoming school year. It was everyone's hope that the article might keep other college kids from making the same mistakes of, not only my daughter, but of sixty-one other students who had lost their lives in fires since 2000. I was glad to do whatever I could to keep families from experiencing the devastating loss of their vibrant, young, adult children.

The morning the article was published, I stopped by the store to buy three copies of the paper. I was eager to read it, but found as I did, that it made me so sad. Liz's picture was included, and the senselessness of her death hit me in a profound way. I should have expected this reaction, but it took me by surprise; it was very difficult dealing with the raw emotion that once again bubbled up and grabbed me. I suddenly wished that the article hadn't been published, that I hadn't emailed family and friends the day before to tell them it would be in today's paper. I threw the paper on the back of the credenza in my office and tried to put it out of my mind. But I couldn't; it was all I could do to keep my composure as my co-workers stopped at my desk to read the article.

It was one of those sad-bad days. I hadn't had one of "those" days in quite some time. "I'll get through it," I told myself, because tomorrow will be better. It was something I have had to deal with many times in the three years since Liz's death. And it always worked. I knew I needed to allow myself to feel the pain before it would leave me.

I tried to put the article out of my mind and focus on my job. I worked in Purchasing/Sales/Customer

Service for a corporation and often was in contact with international customers. Because of the time differences, email was the preferred method of communication. As I was working through the day's emails, a familiar address suddenly popped up. It was Liz's high school French teacher, Jan. Jan had been Liz's favorite teacher, and we'd kept in touch after Liz's death. In fact, I had shared my news about the newspaper article with her, and I was assuming her email was about the article. Much to my surprise, it wasn't.

"Kim," she said, "you will just treasure this. I was cleaning out my files yesterday, getting ready for the new school year. A lone folder fell on the floor. I picked it up and read, 'Liz Wencl Essay' on the cover. I opened it and found a letter she had written to you."

Jan explained that she had given her students this assignment four years earlier: *Write in French a letter to your mother or father and tell them what they represent in your life.*

Jan told me that reading Liz's letter jogged her memory, and she remembered telling Liz how beautiful the letter was. She encouraged Liz to share the letter with me. She even remembered Liz's comment, "I will when the time is right."

That letter was a mother's dream. It said everything I would ever want to hear from my child. She told me how much she loved me and missed me in so many different ways.

Receiving that letter was no coincidence. I believe with all my heart that my daughter is still with me, and on the day the article was published, she knew I was having a difficult day. She reached out to me from heaven to let me know just how much she loves me and misses me, just as I love and miss her.

I plan to have the letter framed. On one side I will have the French version and on the other side the English version. In the middle I will have a photograph of the two of us. It will hang in our hallway and will be a constant reminder of the power of our love. That letter is visual proof for me that Liz reached out and touched me on a day when I really needed it.

I am sure that I will have more sad-bad days in the years to come. But when I do, I will need only to read her letter to feel, once again, the strong bond that we share. It is a bond that cannot be broken, not even by death.

Just as God's love for his children never changes, the love that my daughter and I share never changes. It will live for all eternity.

Here is the English translation of the letter:

Dear Mom,

I know you love me. You show me each day that it is true. Don't think you are a bad Mother. It isn't true. When I look at you I realize how much I am loved.

When you are feeling bad, don't forget that I truly love you. I would like to be able to be a better daughter. We argue sometimes, and that makes me sad. I feel bad and unhappy if you cry.

I remember one time when I was a little girl and you hugged me and said, "I love you so much, Lizzie, little darling. Sit here with me for just a little while." Those ties were so special for me, and you made me so happy. I felt like nothing could ever hurt me. I used to wish that those moments would never end. To be cuddled up next to you like that today would be a dream come true.

Mom, I feel sad when you feel sad. And when you are happy, I am happy! You are my mother, and I would never choose anyone else. Without you I would never be who I am.

I love you with all my heart.

Kisses,

Liz

Kim Wencl

Forty-one Signs of Hope

*As long as there is life, there's the possibility of love.
And where there's love, there's always hope.*

Marianne Williamson

David and Joanne's eighteen-year-old son, Nicholas, died in the horrific night club fire in Rhode Island on February 20, 2003. Since then, they, Nick's brothers, and several friends have received signs from Nick, indicating that he continues to be in their lives.

As a grieving dad, Dave needed to find a way to help himself in grieving for his son. In *41 Signs of Hope*, Dave shares stories of the many ways in which Nick speaks to his loved ones. In my interview with Dave and Joanne, they shared with me that forty-one was Nick's favorite number. Dave writes in his book:

> *From the time he was very young, Nick had what I would describe as an odd connection*

with the number forty-one. For some reason he would notice this number everywhere. When he got in the car, he'd say, "Hey, Dad! Look, it's 2:41." No matter where it was: license plates, house numbers, sales receipts, football jerseys, Nick would let us know.

In the days and weeks following Nick's death, the number forty-one seemed to take on a life of its own. At first the family thought these signs were coincidences, but slowly, they began to realize that there was more to it than coincidence.

For instance, one day while driving, the windshield wipers in Dave's car turned on without his doing it. He had been thinking of Nick, and when he checked the clock in his car, it read forty-one minutes past the hour.

Other signs appeared; just two days after his son's death, Dave, a singer and composer, honored a commitment to perform in a one-man show, but when he tried to sing, his voice broke in grief. And so he asked his son for help. He writes, *"OK, Nick, you're going to help me with this one."* As he spoke the words, suddenly, Dave heard two chimes ringing very clearly. Normally, the chimes rang at 11 p.m. as a toast to all Elk members who had died. But the night Dave was to sing, no one pressed the button to ring the chimes. Dave realized that Nick was signaling him of his presence, his support, and his undying love. Dave writes:

My message is that you, too, can experience these signs; they are there. You just need to hear and see them. The next time you are in a supermarket, and you hear a special song that connects you with a loved one who has passed, stop and listen. When you get a check from a waitress, and it ends in your loved one's lucky number, acknowledge it. When you see a license plate that carries the name of someone who has passed or hear an expression that reminds you of a particular person, say hello.

There is an old phrase, "hiding in plain sight." This is where we find the loved one we miss so much. All we need to do is open our eyes, our minds, and our hearts.

Allie Bird

*It is through the mind in the heart that
contact with eternity is made.*

White Eagle

There are moments in life that are hard to forget.
One such moment was when I, suddenly, felt
Allie's sweet, gentle energy flowing through me. At nine
years of age, Allie had died in a freak accident riding her
beloved horse, Maxine. Months later, while I was sitting in my office talking to Allie's mom about the many
ways in which Allie communicated her thoughts and
feelings to her family, Allie's presence poured through
me. I knew, in those moments, that Allie wanted me to
write about parents who had lost a child, so that they
might find comfort and help in healing their grief.

Allie's mom, Elena, explained that on May 1st,
2004, while they were in the hospital in Atlanta, Allie

had been rushed in for a second emergency surgery. As Elena watched her daughter being wheeled into the operating room, she knew, intuitively, that she would never see her again. "My head got really hot," she told me, "and the heat just traveled down through my body."

Elena's sister, Jill, an ER nurse, was enroute to Atlanta to be with Allie and the family when she, too, experienced a sensation of intense heat throughout her body. Suddenly, she began to cry, sensing that Allie had just died.

But Allie, a joyful and persistent spirit, was not going to stop communicating with her family. Within days, Elena told me of several odd occurrences; she knew it was her Allie communicating with them.

The morning after Allie died, her sister, Kate, caught sight of a little bird while she was making breakfast. The bird flew right up to the back door and stayed there, quietly staring in through the glass. Kate motioned to Elena to come see the bird. Elena thought the funny looking little bird was peculiar, sitting calmly and staring in at them, but Kate said, "Mom, don't you know about birds?" She explained that those who die often choose to give a sign to their loved ones that they are still with them. Elena had never heard this, and she was skeptical, but watched as the bird continued to sit inches away on the other side of the door.

A few days later, Elena's eighteen-year-old nephew, Gary, arrived for the funeral. Allie's dad had a Porsche, and Gary asked if he could go for a ride in the car. As Elena drove her nephew around the block, turning back into the driveway, they heard the incessant chirping, chirping, chirping and squawking of the same little bird that had sat at their back door. Elena explained that Allie had loved her dad's Porsche and frequently teased, asking if she could have the car when she turned sixteen. Elena knew the chirping bird was Allie reminding the entire family that she wanted the Porsche.

Over the next week, Elena and her family, several times, noticed the funny little bird resting in the evergreen tree beside their house. They named it Allie Bird. After some research, they discovered the bird was a Northern Mockingbird, skinny and long with a tail pointing upward. A social, playful bird, it seemed appropriate that Allie would identify with such a bird.

A year later, Elena and her family moved from Atlanta back to Pennsylvania. The move to their new home was difficult for Elena, because it held no memories of Allie. "Allie never ran or played in this house or in the yard," she told me. "It was so hard to be in a house where I had no vivid memories of her."

"For the first several weeks I was really missing Allie, and I missed Allie Bird. Then one afternoon as I was driving down the road, I saw Allie Bird sitting in a tree. She flew right in front of my car, as if to make sure I had seen her. For the next several days, every time I drove down this one section of the road, Allie Bird swooped down in front of me, and I would think, 'Well, why are you hanging out here? Come home!'"

Elena continued, "Then one Sunday morning I was having an exceptionally rough day. I just didn't want to get out of bed. My husband, Bob, came upstairs to ask if I was getting up. I just looked at him, not even wanting to answer him, and rolled over. He went downstairs, knowing that he had to do something to get me up. He told Kate to ask if I wanted breakfast."

"Suddenly, she started yelling, 'Mom, Mom! Come down here! Come down here, quick! You've got to see this. You're not going to believe it.' I knew she probably was making something up to startle me out of bed, but I rolled over and got up."

Reaching the top of the stairs, Elena heard Kate call, "Oh, just forget it! It's too late now."

"What are you talking about?" Elena asked.

"There was a bird flying around the house! Just go back to bed," Kate said in a very frustrated tone.

Later that afternoon, Elena and Bob were walking around the yard, making a list of all the projects they needed to do. When she looked up, she was stunned to see Allie Bird in the tree. "Oh, my goodness! Look!" she cried. "That's Allie Bird!" Bob added, "That's the same bird that was in the house this morning!"

At that moment, Elena realized that her family had been telling the truth earlier—Allie Bird had come right into the house to help get her up!

Elena felt as if all of this was a special gift from Allie.

Nowadays, Allie Bird spends her time between her family's home and the home of her best friend, Melissa. This is fine with Elena, because the moms are best friends too! Every time Elena pulls into Melissa's driveway, Allie Bird squawks and shoots across the front of her car, as if to say "Hi, mom!"

Dancing Lights

*Most of us encounter a great deal more mystery
than we are willing to experience.
Sometimes, knowing life requires us to suspend
disbelief, recognizing that our hard-won knowledge
may only be provisional and that the world may
be quite different than we believe it to be.*

Rachel Naomi Remen, M.D.,
My Grandfather's Blessings

Brenda kissed her son and said goodbye. "Bye, mom. Be back soon!" A short while later she received a phone call telling her that Matthew was dead from a gunshot wound. For the next few years she was overwhelmed with loss and struggled to reclaim her life. Then a second phone call in which she learned that another of her sons, Stephen, had been in a car accident and was being taken to the Intensive Care Unit at the local hospital. She stayed by his side for days, but after receiving a new medication, which his body rejected, he died.

Brenda knew she needed to learn how to live with the loss of her two boys. She was blessed with two other children who depended on her and who were struggling with their own grief. Although her husband and mother were by her side, Brenda felt terribly alone. Her heart was broken. She couldn't concentrate, couldn't sleep, and couldn't work. She was depressed. If it weren't for her other two children, she would wish to die, to join her boys. But she knew she needed to care for the others.

On a hot, humid summer day, Brenda sat with me in my office. She was tearful through most of the session, but between her tears, she talked about how, after Matthew's death, Stephen understood the importance of signs, how essential and comforting they had been.

After Matthew died, whenever a family photo was taken, a large orb floated in the picture where Matthew would have been standing. They were particularly pronounced in the family's Christmas photos where Matthew would have sat opening his gifts.

The Christmas following Matthew's death was a difficult Christmas. Brenda could not bring herself to purchase the usual six foot Christmas tree they always had. It was Matthew's job to cut it down. Though her heart was not into Christmas, her other children insisted they celebrate, so she agreed to a small tree that they placed on a table.

The children decorated the tree with lights and ornaments, and when they, finally, were finished, they all went to bed. The next morning they discovered the tree lying on its side on the floor, the ornaments neatly piled by the tree. They redecorated and secured the tree, but the following morning, they came downstairs,

again, to find the tree on the floor, the lights and ornaments next to it. The third morning, it was the same
thing. Brenda smiled, telling me this story, knowing
that it was Matthew expressing his disappointment in
not having their traditional six-footer.

There were other signs that continued after Stephen
died. Several times Brenda noticed her dogs staring
up into the air or into the corners of the rooms of
her home. She knew they were sensing what she was
unable to see, and she felt certain that her dogs were
aware of the presence of one or both of her boys. She
envied the dogs, because she so wished to feel her sons'
presence.

One evening Brenda went upstairs to get ready for
bed. It was late, around 12:30 a.m. Brenda had a curtain in place of a wooden door, so that her dogs could
easily come and go from the bedroom. As she pulled
the curtain aside to enter the room, she suddenly felt
very uncomfortable and ungrounded. She could see the
room around her but felt detached from it. "The room
seemed foggy and hazy," she told me. "I felt strange
and disorientated. It was a bit like I feel when I am
meditating."

When Brenda walked into the room, she was
stunned to see beams of red light gliding across the
ceiling. She stared in amazement. The rods of red light
were moving and swaying in a way that resembled a
beautiful dance between two people. Weaving around
her, the lights seemed to gently be engaging her in the
dance. She felt weak and confused, and put her head
on the bureau, trying to make sense of what was

happening. Wanting to clear her head, she stepped out of the room to get a breath of fresh air. When she went back in, the lights had disappeared.

As she crawled into bed, she realized, "That was a visit from Matthew and Stephen." Although saddened that she had lost the opportunity to communicate with her sons, she felt pleased and grateful that her boys had found a way to say hi to her.

Over the years, many patients have told me that, initially, they did not realize a loved one was there to visit. Often such visits are confusing or frightening. But once we become aware of the encounters, we are reassured and comforted by the possibility of other visits.

Grace Boy: A Swan's Story

Grief alone has the power to heal.
Grief always works. Grief always heals.

David Kessler and
Elisabeth Kubler-Ross, M.D.,
On Grief and Grieving

G race Boy, a majestic male swan, was cruelly murdered by a known sociopath in our river community. Grace leaves behind a mate, Zoe, and two handsome cygnets, born just weeks before he was killed. Our entire community mourns his death.

I'm sharing this with you, grieving parents in all stages of recovery, because this swan story is a lesson in loss and the power of love. I found a "soul mate" in Grace Boy during the summer of 2003 when his first mate disappeared within a month of my losing my twenty-three-year-old daughter, Allyson.

We adopted Allyson in Bogota, Columbia at three weeks of age. Bouncy, creative, and strong willed,

Allyson was filled with a bold laughter and spontaneity. Her friends were drawn to her bright light and dazzling smile. However, by her late teens, we began to notice the looming presence of a mood disorder that robbed her of her sense of confidence and well being. Her suicide was not a planned act but a lethal mix of unregulated impulse, severe mood swings consistent with a bipolar disorder, and the presence of a firearm in her apartment.

In the months following her death, my mind whirled with memories of this shining light in my life. It was during this time that Grace Boy became a friendly and soothing presence to me. The loss of his mate reflected my own feelings of deep grief.

For the next four years, neighbors faithfully fed and nurtured this lovely swan, and we continued to share the waters with him as we watched his lonely moments, especially in winter when the ducks, with whom he flocked, abandoned their posts to fly south. During these winter months, Grace drifted offshore in total solitude. His image mirrored my own as I, too, drifted along without my beloved daughter whose presence had imbued my life with a central focus and meaning that could not be replaced by anyone. I felt a deep kinship with Grace Boy.

A miracle happened this past fall; a female flew over our community, and Grace pursued her in flight. Lucky for all of us, the female swan noticed the handsome male and chose to land in our waters where she was courted for the next week. On their wedding day I was lucky to be present, by chance, as they drifted past our dock with their long necks entwined. By spring, another miracle—a mating, a nest and four large eggs! Grace and Zoe worked diligently at being good parents, although despite their efforts, only three of the eggs hatched. Later, one small baby disappeared after a night of nesting onshore. Again my heart ached for the adult swans. How well I knew their grief. The hard work of parenting comes with no guarantee. Yet they set about their tasks with great energy so that they could provide for the two remaining young ones.

Seeing this graceful family brought me such joy, and I hoped it would keep me going through the fifth anniversary of Allyson's death on May 26th and her birthday, August 5th. It was not to be. The lovely swan family, whole and happy, was fractured by the death of the proud and protective father.

Why must we endure these vast holes in our lives created by the untimely passing of our beloved children? How can we go on? Can we ever recover? When will the pain lessen? Who can help us to cope? Can we help ourselves? I am still asking these questions after five years but believe there are answers in the story of Grace Boy.

Grace's home was the Delaware River, a ribbon of water separating New Jersey and Pennsylvania. River folks share common values and priorities: the sanctity of life transcends all our differences and binds us together. Grace's death underscored our need to form common bonds of love, respect, and caring for one another, just as our river, teeming with wildlife, reminds us to find joy in every moment that we are alive in the midst of God's grand creatures.

Grace's death has renewed our strength and reminded us that in talking with our neighbors, we all seek the shelter of each other. Our goal is to support one another and to support our wildlife family. Look around you at all living creatures. Make your life count by alleviating suffering and celebrating the joys of these living creatures.

Allyson's death challenges me to make sense of our path. We rebuild our identities one brick at a time, struggling with guilt and our responsibility as parents. The healing process begins by allowing ourselves to ask the questions that really bring us to our knees. Did my child really understand that I would have given my own life rather than lose her?

But with time we begin to reclaim our lives. Losing a child is the most difficult challenge life brings, but we learn to take solace from the world around us—the beauty and the heartache. All we can do is go forward, alleviating what suffering we can, supporting and celebrating the joys in the life that surrounds us.

Trish Myers

2

Losing a Parent

*We are seasoned by each other's lives.
Our joy and sorrows are woven into
the tapestry of shared history.*

LINDA ELLERBY

The Embrace

Love may speak a language all its own
But true love seldom needs an interpreter.

Maya Angelou

It had been four months since my mother's passing. Her illness was sudden, and she was spared a lengthy deterioration. I was heartbroken, having lost both my parents within three years. But I had mastered the art of remaining detached, focusing on others and my work. I suppressed my emotions, but I was like a volcano on the verge of eruption.

My sister is eleven years younger than I. She was born prematurely, weighing only one pound at birth, and it was truly a miracle that she survived, her frail little body strengthening into a lovely teenager. My parents, understandably, sheltered and protected their "baby" girl, and during my mother's illness, she worried more about her "baby" than her own health and passing.

I promised my mother that after she died I would take care of my sister. I lived in New Jersey but planned to move back to South Philly after having been gone for eight years. I was glad to honor my commitment to my mother and ensure that my little sister stayed on the right track. July 21st was my moving day.

It was a hot, steamy day. The movers arrived with my furniture and cartons of stuff, but the furniture was oversized and wouldn't fit through the narrow stairways of our South Philadelphia row house. I had been the tower of strength, holding it together for everyone, but suddenly my emotions started to soar out of control. Standing in the living room I felt a strange feeling envelop me; a feeling reminiscent of a dense fog clouded my brain as I began to melt. It reminded me of the witch in *The* Wizard *of Oz* screaming "I'm melting" after Dorothy drenched her with the bucket of water. Frozen, I heard the phone ring. It was my sister, who noticed the distant tone and kept asking, "What's wrong?" I didn't know.

Sinking into my mother's favorite loveseat, I curled into a fetal position. The tears flowed; my heart was filled with an immense and indescribable sadness. Lying there with my eyes closed, I felt a presence embrace me. It was soft, gentle and comfortable.

I had never experienced anything like this before, but I wasn't afraid. I sensed the presence and found myself calmed as my tears stopped. The soft, feminine energy began to rock me as a mother would rock her fretting child. I didn't open my eyes but accepted the sustained embrace as it rocked me to sleep. It seemed that the angels knew I finally was breaking down and needed the comfort and support I'd given others. I awoke restored.

Linda Marshall

$\mathcal{L}$esson One: God is Real

This is God talking and he's saying,
"You would not be seeking me
If you had not already found me."

Morrie Schwartz

Hearing the doctor say "You have cancer." was merely an affirmation of what my father already suspected. It was June 1984, and I had been living in Dallas, Texas but had accepted a new job in Kansas City. Before starting my new position, I took time off to visit my family seventeen hundred miles away in Philadelphia.

Walking in the door, I immediately noticed that my dad had lost a tremendous amount of weight. But it didn't slow him down; up early the next morning, he prepared his famous breakfast of home-fries, sausage, and fish for everyone. We sat at the table devouring the delicious meal, but he ate nothing. I was concerned and asked him how he was feeling. Before I left for Kansas, I insisted that we visit his doctor, and it was then that his doctor confirmed the "c" word.

The doctor wanted him hospitalized immediately, but my dad refused. Being a man's man, he possessed tremendous pride, and he felt a deep commitment to me, which meant that he wanted, as usual, to pack my car for the long road trip. That ritual cemented his role as father and protector. He also didn't want me leaving with images of him lying in a hospital bed. However, he did promise that once he saw me on the road, he would follow his doctor's advice and admit himself to the hospital.

His cancer was advanced. Although he always had been in great shape, he was a lifelong smoker. Unfortunately, surgery of the lung and his esophagus offered no respite, and he died within six months.

This was my first experience of losing someone I loved deeply. During his illness my nights and private moments were filled with tears and prayers. The anticipation and reality of losing a parent were absolutely inconceivable. I had been taught that God answers prayers, and that miracles were possible. But when none came our way, when my dad finally died, I was pissed at God.

I couldn't imagine a reality in which I would never see him again, never hear his voice or his laugh, and never feel his embrace. There was a hole in our family. Sadness and anger enveloped me and was exacerbated by seeing my mom's grief. I masked my feelings but went to church with the express purpose of letting God know that I was angry and no longer trusted him. I hadn't asked for much, so why had he failed me?

One night, deep in sleep, I experienced what I came to realize was a visitation. My father appeared at the foot of my bed, suspended in air in a beautiful glowing light. He looked healthy, his demeanor calm and loving. We began a dialogue I will never forget.

"Daddy, it's you. Are you OK?"

"Linda, I am fine. I'm OK. Don't be angry with God."

I asked, "Is God real?" to which he responded, "Yes, he is, but he is not what you think or what you've been taught."

I didn't think God could forgive my blasphemous, hateful attitude, but my dad reassured me.

"Don't be angry. It's not too late to be forgiven. You have time."

The image of my dad faded, and I fell back into a deep sleep. The next morning when I woke, I was excited and called my mom to share my dream and my dad's message. My mom accepted my story without question or doubt. She, too, had often shared stories of her dreams in which messages were delivered. Both she and my father had what old folks called "being born with a veil." She assured me that my dad, who often stressed that I needed to manage my anger, had come to deliver that message. He understood that anger is a debilitating emotion, and he defied the laws of nature to ensure that I heard his voice.

His visitation had a profound impact on my life and proved to be the start of my spiritual quest. I wanted to know "God." The good book says to "Seek and ye shall find." God, Source, Spirit are everywhere, and I am forever grateful for my father who pushed me through anger to a powerful and fulfilling path of exploration!

Linda Marshall

The Yartzheit Candle

Where there is love, there is life.

Ghandi

Natalie Kaye remembers, with great clarity, the events surrounding the death of her mom. It was the day before Thanksgiving, and two weeks before Natalie was to move into a new home. She was stunned and overwhelmed by grief.

"We are of the Jewish faith," she explained, "and our family decided to sit Shiva from Friday through Sunday in my parents' home in New York." Sitting Shiva is a Jewish ritual in which family members of the deceased sit at home as other family and friends come to pay their respects and offer support in a time of grief.

When Natalie returned home to Pennsylvania, she sat Shiva in her own house for another three days, but because she had not had the chance to call her friends to tell them of her mother's death, she had no visitors, and no one to comfort her.

Sitting alone, she became distraught about having to move within two weeks. Out of love and loyalty for her mom, she did not pack but became increasingly anxious and agitated. On the third day, however, as she walked downstairs to sit for the final day of Shiva, she heard an odd noise, a sharp splitting or crack. She went to check on the Yartzheit candle, a tall candle that burns for a week following the death of a loved one. What she saw stunned her! There, on the dining room table was the candle, and it had cracked, exactly in the middle. "This was unheard of and so unusual," she said. "I didn't know what to do." What she did decide to do was to stop sitting Shiva and begin to pack.

Later that afternoon a friend telephoned to tell Natalie that her mom had come to her with a message: "Tell Natalie that she does not have to sit Shiva anymore. She has packing that she must do. I do not want her to sit. I want her to pack and get ready for the move!"

Natalie laughed as she listened to her friend relating her mom's message. "That got me through the period of loss and mourning for my mom. And the cracked Yartzheit candle really got my attention. Both were very healing for me."

Natalie enjoyed a wonderful relationship with her mother, and though her mom was not demonstrative, she showed her love for Natalie in many caring ways. "While my mom was dying I was able to spend a month with her, which deepened our relationship. In fact, I was there when my mom took her last breath, and I watched as she moved into another dimension."

There were others ways that Natalie's mom demonstrated her love for her. Natalie was to decide when to take her mom off life support, but just as Natalie's husband, Ivan, arrived at the hospital, Natalie's mom died. Natalie believes that her mom chose to die so as to spare Natalie from making the decision. She also believes that her mom chose to leave once she was assured that Ivan was there with Natalie so that Natalie would not be alone.

"I feel her loving support and protection," she says. "I feel so fortunate and believe our relationship is closer than ever. She is always around—on Mother's Day, my birthday, her birthday, holidays. Something always reminds me of her. I put together an album of her life. When I miss her, I look through it and always feel better."

Bless Those Green Eyes

There is a land of the living and a land of the dead,
And the bridge is love, the only
survival, the only meaning.

Thornton Wilder,
The Bridge of San Luis Rey

We walked into Joseph's room with his wife, LouLou, who happened to come onto the hospital floor at the same time. Joseph, battling Non-Hodgkin's Lymphoma, was noticeably thinner than when we last had been together, but I was delighted to see the color in his face. His face was a bit flushed, and his smile told me he was pleased to see us. He seemed to have a bit of an appetite and was watching the Olympics on television when we walked in.

We pulled chairs up to his bed and stayed for an hour, chatting about the Olympics and his hospital stay, and when the conversation turned more serious, about the long, extensive, healing journey he was experiencing.

Not wanting to wear him out, we finally said goodbye. LouLou walked with us to the elevator and downstairs to the front of the hospital where our car was parked. She told us how much better Joseph looked and seemed from the day before.

LouLou noted that the day before was August 14th, the one month anniversary of the death of Joseph's 102 year-old mother. LouLou wondered aloud if there could be a relationship between the date of his mother's death and the significant improvement in his health exactly four weeks later. And if so, was it possible that his mother had found a way, energetically, to help her son feel better?

In my book, *Touched by the Extraordinary,* I discuss a phenomenon called "enmeshment" in which deceased loved ones lovingly infuse their energy into our beings by merging with us, often when we are running low physically and emotionally.

On the evening we were visiting Joseph in the hospital, LouLou commented on how green Joseph's eyes seemed to have become. Although they always had had a touch of green in them, they previously were more hazel. But since his mom had died, the green had become brighter and more noticeable.

Months later, LouLou told me that Joseph also had begun to take on the same mannerisms, tone of voice, and gestures as his mom's. Recently, when eating a peach, she'd been stunned to hear him exclaim "DELICIOUS!" as he bit into the flesh. She spun around, "I could have sworn it was his mother," she said, the intonation and expression identical.

"It is amazing how similar his mannerisms are to his mother's," she told me. She added that now when he looks at her, it is with his eyes wide open, as his mother often had.

LouLou continues to notice and wonder. She is well aware that life is filled with extraordinary moments.

Oneness

*Any separation from each other is an
optical illusion of consciousness.*

Albert Einstein

My dear, sweet, friend and editor, Bev, died in December 2008 during the season's first snow fall. Bev and her husband, Dan, had a son who died at twenty-seven. Their other two children, Mike and Val, and their granddaughter, Audrey, were unable to make it to Bev's bedside to say goodbye because of the bad weather.

Val is no stranger to death and dying. Not only did she lose her brother, but as an adult, devoted her life to helping those in hospice care experience their final days feeling as comfortable as possible. A hospice nurse with years of inpatient experience, now a complimentary therapy hospice and palliative care nurse and coordinator, Val works alongside a team of end-of-life professionals. She has supported over eight thousand patients and families in her hospice nursing position. Her interest is in the use of holistic therapies that ease stress and the effects of fear. Her teachings are shared nationally. She tries to achieve peace in every sense of the word, and lives and breathes her work.

But even Val, with her years of experience, was deeply moved by her mother's unique way of saying "I love you." According to Val, the morning after her mom died, she and Audrey were driving to Connecticut to be with her brother and her dad. While she was driving she felt a tingling rush across her back, a feeling she often had experienced when thinking of a patient who recently died.

Val and Bev often talked about death, Bev promising to come to Val with a sign. As Val was driving to Connecticut, she silently told her mom, "Channel, if it is you . . . I can." Within the next few minutes Val felt her mother's energy moving through her.

The experience was painful for Val. She felt her mom's energy deep within her, and that closeness heightened her sense of grief. She tried very hard to hear what her mom was saying to her. Suddenly, she heard herself speaking, "I love you all so much. I love you and Audrey so very, very much."

Val turned to Audrey asking, "What just happened?"

Audrey stunned and in tears said, "You looked and sounded just like Ammie. Your face changed. You looked older and more wrinkled . . . and sad . . . . like when Ammie is crying." Listening to Audrey, Val knew that her mother, with a powerful loving energy, had spoken through her. By becoming one with her daughter, Bev chose to be present in the most special way. Her loving communication with Val and Audrey brought them each comfort and hope.

A Father's Presence

When one believes in miracles,
divine intervention can occur.

Bernie Siegel, M.D.

It was Saturday, the day before Mother's Day. I woke thinking of my father. He had died the previous Christmas, three and one half months earlier, and I was in the throes of deep grief. But as I dressed, I noticed the clear, warm, spring day. My children were coming in for the weekend so that we could celebrate Mother's Day together, and I had been given a gift certificate for a massage. After I dressed, I drove off for my appointment with my massage therapist, Jodi York, feeling a sense of peace.

While Jodi worked her healing magic on my body, massaging away the aches in my back and shoulders, she whispered that my father was present. I was so grateful to hear this as I missed him very much.

As I was leaving her office, she told me, "Remember, Susan, you will be receiving roses today, and when you receive them, know that they actually are coming from your father."

I thanked Jodi. Her words touched me, as did the thought of my dad, but as I hurried home these thoughts left me, and I turned my attention to all the chores I needed to do before my children arrived.

While I was in the garden pulling weeds and planting bulbs, I saw the UPS truck drive up. The delivery man ran a long green box up to the door and placed it on the doorstep. When I finished in the garden, I picked up the box and took it with me into the kitchen, placing it on the counter near my desk. I didn't give a thought to Jodi's earlier words and left the box there while I went to cleanup. Only later did I remember to open it.

Pulling away layers of delicate paper shreds, I unearthed a bouquet of exquisite roses—first, a pink one, then a sunny yellow, a lovely, peach rose, and finally, a beautiful, pure, white one. Their fragrance filled my kitchen as I placed the roses in a vase of water. When I read the card I saw the flowers were from Mary, the gentle soul who lovingly had cared for my dad after my mom died.

Only then did I remember Jodi's words, "You will receive roses today." I realized that Dad, of course, would send roses through Mary. I was filled with gratitude and love, and through my tears, thanked him for finding a way to communicate with me and reassuring me I am not alone.

The power of a rose can say so much. Roses, I have found, are often a way for deceased loved ones to express their love. In the way that Mary became the conduit for my father to connect with me, I also became a conduit for a good friend who lives in England. This past January, I felt an impulse to send her a bouquet of roses. She called to thank me and told me that the day she received them she had been feeling sad, thinking about and missing her father, who had died the year before. During his life, he frequently sent her roses, and she knew, when she saw the big box from Harrods arriving at her door, that the roses were from me and her father.

Roses are a symbol of love and a testament to the fact that love does not die. Rather, love empowers, heals, and provides us with hope.

3

Loss of a Spouse

Love is our true destiny.
We do not find the meaning of life by ourselves alone.
We find it with one another.

THOMAS MERTON

Snowfall, Lights

Love, like hope, heals.
It is the very foundation of prayer.
If we allow hope to mingle with love,
the problem of false hope will evaporate.

Larry Dossey, M.D.

Patients who grieve their spouses have shared with me the pain of losing their identity, of not knowing who they are, and of no longer knowing what their purpose is. They tell me how difficult it is to come home to an empty house, how much they miss talking with their loved one, how unbearably lonely life is, even when they are with old friends.

Often, however, they feel the presence of their spouses. Lights will blink at the moment they are thinking of their spouse, or the television will turn on, often to one of their favorite programs.

Sometimes, while in the car, a special song will come on the radio.

What I especially love are the stories they share about being in bed; in the months following the death of their spouse, many of my patients report that they will sense fingers lightly touching their forehead, or will feel a delicate breeze gently passing over their face or neck, or can sense the presence of someone lying next to them. They tell me they *know* their spouse is there, with them, to sooth and comfort them.

This loving presence often comes in dreams in which a spouse comes to say hello or leave a message. There also are other signs and indications they are present.

One of my favorite stories is that of Elizabeth Kubler-Ross, a psychiatrist and researcher on death and afterlife. In her autobiography, *The Wheel of Life,* she writes of her ex-husband, Manny, who was dying. He was skeptical of her beliefs in an eternal life, but she asked that when he died to please provide her with a signal that life continued after death. Standing at his gravesite it began to snow, but all around her on the ground were roses. She picked them up and handed one to her daughter, Barbara, who reminded Elizabeth of a conversation in which Manny said, "If what your mother says is true (that life continues after death), then during the first snowfall after my death, there will be red roses blooming in the snow." As she recalled his words, Elizabeth smiled and quietly thanked her husband for confirming her beliefs that life continues after death.

My own father, a traditional, old-fashioned doctor also believed that "it is real only if you can see it, touch it or feel it." However, after my mom's death, he began to consider the possibility that she, in fact, was trying to connect with him. On the day of her funeral, an icy, snowy bitter cold day, we returned home from the cemetery where she was buried. There were many people in the house and a great deal of commotion, but we noticed that the kitchen light was blinking. It continued to blink for more than a half an hour, although the light bulb, plug, and outlet were secure.

In the years that followed my mom's death, often when my dad arrived home, the television would turn on to his favorite station. He took the television to be repaired, but it continued to flick on, as though to say hello and welcome home.

This brought my dad great comfort, thinking that perhaps my mom was with him, aware of his feelings of love for her and sadness in her death.

My heart goes out to those who grieve their spouses. It is a part of life, as is the loss of parents, children, and other family members. But the period after a loved one's death is profoundly challenging, often filled with long periods of transitional adjustment, growth, and eventually, recognition that it is possible to go on.

We are all in this together. Remember to be compassionate to those who have lost their partners, in the same way that we would want others to extend to us the same compassion.

That Face

Some people, no matter how old they
get, never lose their beauty.
They merely move it from their faces into their hearts.

Martin Buxbaum

It was a beautiful fall Monday. The air was crisp, and the leaves had started to turn into vibrant shades of orange and yellow. Michael was on his way to visit his son when he saw a familiar face. He slowed his car, rolled down his window, and called out to the gentleman sweeping leaves into a pile by the driveway. "Hi there, Sam! How are you?"

Michael did not know Sam well, but over the years, he had become good friends with Sam's wife, Ann. Every Friday Ann came into Michael's store to shop. Sometimes Sam came with her, and the two men nodded hello or exchanged a few words, but usually they just went about their business. Michael was very fond of Ann and liked her elderly, kind husband.

When Ann was diagnosed with cancer, she fought her illness with great dignity and strength, and when she died, Michael felt the loss of her friendship and a real emptiness. He could not imagine the deep grief that Sam felt in losing his lifelong love. Michael prayed for both Ann and Sam's souls.

As Michael called over to Sam, Sam turned smiling, both men surprised and genuinely pleased to see one another. When Michael asked Sam how he was doing, Sam replied that he was in the process of selling his house. "It is just too much house for me without my Ann," he told Michael. "I've bought a small condominium and will be moving there so that I will be closer to my children."

As Sam was talking, sunlight flooding his face, Michael noticed that Sam's features were beginning to change shape, to take a different form. Michael was stunned to realize that Ann's face was emerging through Sam's. It was as if she was coming to say hello to her old friend, Michael. "Oh, my God," he thought to himself. "It's Ann." Mystified, he found himself speaking silently to her, reassuring her that he knew she was present for him and for her beloved Sam.

Within minutes, Ann's face disappeared, and Sam's features returned. Michael was moved by the event and felt blessed to have received such a gift.

In *Touched by the Extraordinary,* there is a discussion on "enmeshment, a process in which a deceased loved one's energy merges with the physical being who is deeply grieving them. It is a way to provide needed strength and comfort, to soothe and to lessen the grief.

Ann chose this particular process to give strength and comfort to her husband and to say hello to her old friend, Michael.

Each Day

True love is always a risk. But the universe isn't invested just in giving us what we want. It's invested in teaching us how to love.

Marianne Williamson

Life is filled with choices, but the key question is: do we choose to live a life founded on love? Science has validated the power of love. And many of us, even without the science, know that what matters most to us is love.

Not long ago I heard, through the internet, a story that demonstrates the beauty and power of love.

An older gentleman had a doctor's appointment. While in the office speaking to his doctor, he mentioned that he was worried about getting to his next appointment, a visit to the nursing home where his wife lived. His wife had Alzheimer's and had not recognized him in five years, but the man visited her every day.

The doctor was surprised by the man's insistence that he be on time, given that his wife did not remember him. The man explained, "She does not know me, but I still know who she is." The doctor, in an article she later wrote, noted how touched she was by the man's deep love for his wife. She wrote that she, too, hoped one day to find such love. She wrote, "True love is neither physical nor romantic. True love is acceptance of all that is, all that has been, will be, and will not be."

Love is the reason we are here. How many of us would have chosen to love in the way that he did? Choose wisely, each day, because the very heart of your existence rests on your choices.

A Bird Calls

Two songs it has, and both of them I've heard:
I did not know those strains of joy and sorrow
Came from one throat, or that each note could borrow
Strength from the other, making one more brave
And one as sad as rain-drops on the grave.

George Parsons Lathrop

The bird arrived in early spring, when Bev was still well, and throughout the season, while working in the garden or sitting at the kitchen table having coffee, she and Dan were captivated by the distinct two-note call. At first they thought the bird to be a Northern Mockingbird, but after researching it, knew that it was some other songbird, unknown to them in eastern Pennsylvania. It seemed to inhabit the edge of the woods near the barn, and its endless call—first a sharp, clear chirp, then a rasping stutter—went unanswered; perhaps it was alone and without a mate.

By late summer, Bev and Dan retired to their cottage in Connecticut, and it was there they were welcomed by the familiar whistle. After months of trying to identify the bird, they discovered it was an eastern Phoebe, a small, grayish-brown bird with a tail that wagged continuously. The bird foraged by the woods and the water, and its "fee-beee" song delighted them, as they unpacked cartons of books and dishes.

Most forest songbirds leave during the peak of migration in mid-October, but Bev and Dan's Phoebe was late in leaving, hanging on until the bitter cold of November had set in. By then, Bev had weakened, and in December, a few days before Christmas, she died. It was a Friday evening around seven, and a fierce snow-storm was barreling up the coast, making it impossible for the funeral home to get to the hospice center. Dan asked the nursing staff if he could stay with Bev's body until morning.

In the still hours of the night, Dan's heart quick-ened when he suddenly heard the bright two-note song of a Phoebe very close to him, coming from the right of the room. There was silence, then twenty minutes later, a second call from the left. In the darkness he lis-tened to several more calls, the last few becoming more distant, then again silence.

As a chemical engineer, Dan knew there had to be some natural law to explain the sound. He'd spent a life-time working with pipes and pressures, and he checked the heating vents in the room to see if he could explain, physically, the sounds he'd heard. But he had listened carefully, and he knew they were not mechanical sounds. He knew it was his dearest friend and love, who late this past summer again called to him from the branches of a white pine, torn by wind but quivering with life.

4

Loss of a Friend

Don't be dismayed by goodbyes.
A farewell is necessary before you can meet again.
And meeting again, after moments or lifetimes,
is certain for those who are friends.

RICHARD BACH

Orange Gerbera Daisies

*The experience of suffering and the wisdom
we may find there will be completely our
own. Often it will help us live better.
Sometimes, it may help us die better as well*

Rachel Naomi Remen, M.D.,
My Grandfather's Blessings

I lost a very dear friend, Emily, to cancer this past weekend. She was only forty-two-years-old and died on the eve of her baby boy's second birthday. She also leaves behind a five-year-old daughter who is just beginning kindergarten. Emily and her husband found love a bit later than many, but were grateful for the perfect family they had created. They recently celebrated their sixth wedding anniversary. Less than a year ago, however, Emily was diagnosed with end-stage colon cancer.

I met Emily in person only one time. We came to know one another through a message board online. It is a small message board comprised of moms from all walks of life who live scattered across the United States, as well as some who live abroad. Most of us have been friends for more than eight years; we feel very close to one another and have shared our joys and our heartaches, as we would with friends who live down the block.

Emily had a deep faith and fought her cancer, trying against all odds to survive at least for a few more years so that she might be with her children. As her friends, we supported her in her battle. We created a schedule so that each week she received a card in the mail from someone on the board. We raised money to help cover costs of her staggering medical treatments. We also helped to provide food and gifts for last year's Christmas. We held online prayer vigils and prayed for a miracle.

Her death devastated us. It seemed so unfair; it was unimaginable to think that her babies had lost their mommy. The anguish in our voices was gut-wrenching, and none of us knew how to cope with this loss of our beloved, long-time friend, and member of our community. How do you mourn online, when you cannot reach out to hug your friends?

While I was at work today, my husband went to the grocery store for me. He had seen my tears and knew how upset I was over Emily. My husband loves roses and often buys me a bouquet. But today, while he was at the store, he felt drawn to a particular bouquet of orange gerbera daisies. He couldn't explain why he'd chosen these particular flowers, but he wanted to bring them to me to cheer me up.

When I got home from work and found the vase of daisies on our table, I began to weep. My husband was distraught, thinking something was wrong. When I gathered myself together, I told him that I was weeping for joy. The daisies were a sign that Emily was okay.

Emily's signature on our message board was a painting of a single orange gerbera daisy. She began posting the painting after her diagnosis. Underneath the daisy is the message "Find Beauty Every Day." All of us on the message board think of orange gerbera daisies as Emily's flower.

I had never told my husband this. I know that Emily was sending us a signal, and I believe she already is an angel. I posted a photo of the bouquet and the story behind it to my friends, and all of us have found great comfort in it. Truly, there is no other reason for my husband, knowing I needed comfort, to have bought the daisies rather than his favorite roses. He told me the bouquet was sitting alone in a bucket, one of a kind, and he found the orange gerberas to be so beautiful. Even in death, Emily encourages us to find beauty in every day.

Janie Hermann

Ladybugs

*In order to become a realist,
you must believe in miracles.*

David Ben-Gurion

It was four o'clock in the morning, October 30th, 2005. Amy and I were sitting by Chris' bedside along with Chris' husband, Bob, her brother, Danny, and her sister-in-law, Kate.

Chris had been placed on hospice care the day before. During the afternoon, we'd promised her that we would honor whatever sign she chose to let us know that she was with us. Now, sitting with her, we knew her body was failing and her death imminent. There was a visible difference in her breath—a regular but labored breath. We dozed off and on. Danny felt Chris' familiar touch on his scalp, as if she were running her fingers through his hair.

As dawn broke, we looked up at the ceiling to see a beautiful ladybug directly over Chris. Danny called it the "Lady Bird Beetle" and felt it was a sign; Chris was letting us know that her spirit was leaving her body and was free. She wanted us to know she was OK.

For two more days her body held on to every breath. But on Wednesday, Chris' body let go, and her spirit was eternally freed. I was in the hall of my office when my secretary told me, "Dr. Harvey is on the phone." Knowing what the call was about, I walked to my desk, and as I sat down, I saw a ladybug under my desk. I began to cry as I picked up the phone to talk to Amy. I told her Chris was letting me know that she was with me. I could feel her presence.

Several days later, while I was home organizing my house, I went into my study and saw ladybugs scattered all over my curtains, windows, and desk. I called Amy, and with tears in my eyes, told her about the infestation. She also was crying, because she too had just found ladybugs all over her kitchen. Her cats were batting them playfully around the room. We both were so thankful for Chris' messages and loved the way she had chosen to let us feel her presence. When I returned to my study, the ladybugs had disappeared.

On Saturday before the Memorial Service, again the ladybugs came back, a sign from my friend that she was with me. With every sighting I called Amy; she too received the same ladybug messages.

On Tuesday November 14th, we gathered to celebrate the life of Christine O'Donnell. It was a beautiful ceremony that Chris had planned. Amy and I sat together, and during Danny's eulogy, a ladybug kept flying around Danny's head. He swatted it away, at one point. I think Chris was trying to tell him to keep it short and sweet, but Danny spoke for a long while, honoring Chris and her remarkable life.

Chris had chosen one of the readings for the service, Corinthians 15:42–44, to show us the true nature of spirit. Her brother, Paul, read:

This is how it will be when the dead are raised to life. When the body is buried it is mortal; when it is raised, it will be immortal. When buried, it is ugly and weak; when raised, it will be beautiful and strong. When buried, it is a physical body; when raised, it will be a spiritual body. There is, of course, a physical body, so there has to be a spiritual body.

In the weeks following the Memorial Service, the weather became colder. I expected the ladybugs to disappear, and although none surfaced in other parts of my house, I did find two single ones in my study— Chris letting me feel her presence.

I traveled to Cincinnati in early December. The weather had turned bitter cold, twenty-eight degrees outside. I was having dinner at a friend's house and was responsible for making pomegranate martinis. It was a new recipe. I poured vodka and pomegranate juice into a pitcher and took an orange, cutting it in half and squeezing the juice into the mix. As I stirred the ingredients together, I realized the navel end of the orange had fallen into the pitcher and scooped it out with my spoon. You guessed it—a ladybug! Of course, I called Amy immediately, while my friend, Alison, found a raisin for the ladybug to munch on. I told her my story, and when her daughter came in and started to pick up the lady bug, Alison said, "Careful honey, that is Beth's friend, Chris!" Something was lost in the translation, or else it was the martinis, but we all had a good laugh.

Back home, I continued to find ladybugs, one beneath a stack of resumes for positions at our new hospital, Chris, clearly, showing her support for our new venture.

Another day, as I walked into the room to see a patient on a clinical trial, the coordinator, who always addresses me as Dr. DuPree, looked up and said, "Hello, Ladybug." She quickly apologized, "I am so sorry. I don't know why I called you that, except that it is my daughter's nickname."

"Don't be sorry," I said. "You are just giving me a message from a dear friend."

As the Christmas holidays approached, I decided to find a small token gift for Amy to remind her of our ladybug visits. I searched the small shops in Newtown but couldn't find the critters anywhere. On the Monday before Christmas, my watched stopped. On my way home from work, I stopped at the jewelers for a new battery. As I was leaving I noticed, in a small case, a bracelet with true-to-size ladybugs. The sales person commented that it was a child's bracelet, but when he brought it out of the display case, he realized it was sized for adults. They found a second bracelet in the stockroom, so now Amy and I have our ladybugs with us every day!

Dr. Beth DuPree

Kerry and the Dog Food

The first duty of love is to listen.

Paul Tillich

My high school tennis partner, Kerry, was diagnosed with metastatic lung cancer in early 2006. Despite her valiant effort and the best chemotherapy, radiation therapy, and holistic services, she passed into spirit the following October.

I had not seen Kerry for years when she contacted me. We rekindled our friendship, and she told me that she had read my book, *The Healing Consciousness: A Doctor's Journey to Healing,* and felt that I had written it for her at just the right moment in her life.

Kerry had always been stubbornly independent and found it difficult to ask for help. But her journey with cancer awakened her essence, and she became very open to complimentary healing techniques. I shared several Reiki sessions with her that helped her to heal many wounds from this lifetime.

The day before she passed, I visited her at home. She was lying in bed peacefully. Her two dogs stood guard by her side. Although she was slipping in and out of consciousness and unable to speak, I promised her, as I have many others, I will be open to messages she sends from the other side.

Kerry never had children, but her dogs were her loves. She was worried about what would happen to them when she passed. After her funeral, her friends discussed what to do. Her boyfriend, Bob, had planned to keep the dogs and buy the house where they had been living, but he was unable to do this. I considered taking them to my farm, but I already had two dogs, two boys and wasn't sure I could take on another two dogs.

Oddly, during the next few weeks, I began to find dog food in the oddest places—in my shoes, in my filing cabinets, in the pockets of my coats. At first, my family and I blamed it on mice, a logical guess, since we live in an old stone farmhouse. But then we realized that the dog food I was finding was not the same brand that our dogs ate.

I told my friend, Jan, about it, and she burst out laughing. She told me that Kerry probably wanted me to have the dogs and was sending me a sign. She suggested that the family look for an extended family member to take the dogs. Happily, the family was able to place the dogs on a farm in Virginia with one of

Kerry's cousins. And of course, as soon as the dogs had settled into their new life on the farm, the dog food findings stopped.

Our loved ones can always reach us; we just need to listen carefully, as the messages are not always ones we can hear!

Dr. Beth DuPree

$\mathcal{A}$ Gift from Kerry

We die not because we are ill but
because we are complete.
Illness is the occasion of our dying, but not the cause.

A Tibetan Lama

Kerry passed peacefully and was buried in our home town. I was unable to attend her memorial service, but I sent a letter, which our friend, Jan, read at the service.

Kerry wouldn't want us to cry or grieve. We all know Kerry would ask us to raise our glasses and propose a toast to our girlfriend. If given the choice between a church service and the pizza party at Vito's Pizza, hands down she would have chosen the pizza party.

I reminded Kerry just a few weeks ago during a Reiki session we shared that this time will be difficult for those she leaves behind. She truly was not afraid of dying, as she embraced the eternal nature of her soul. I know she no longer is in pain, no longer suffering, and is now free in spirit to soar.

We come together to celebrate her life today and to support her mother, Janice, her sister, Susan, her brother, Eddie, Bob, the man she loved, and all of her friends from every time in her life.

It is often difficult to make sense of death when it comes so prematurely. There is no going back to change the things in our past that we wish we could alter. Kerry grew spiritually in the past months and shared with us her new awakening. Realization of her mortality allowed her to become fully aware of each and every moment. She had several experiences in which she felt the presence of her father, Fred. I am sure he was waiting with open arms to embrace his baby girl, and I know this was a comfort for Kerry. She believed her father was responsible for bringing Bob into her life. She told me how much Bob's unconditional love for her helped her to truly love herself.

She began to find dimes everywhere on her journey (as did her family and friends), and she pondered their significance. Was it a sign that she had ten more years? Was it a sign that the tenth month would be significant? Was it a sign from her dad that she was right on the money about the eternal nature of her soul when a beautiful butterfly landed smack in the middle of a dime? It is not about the interpretation; it's about Kerry's acceptance that she was a spiritual being having a human experience.

In the months and weeks preceding her passing, she felt the presence of her father, and this brought her great comfort. She welcomed being reconnected with him, yet felt compelled to fight as hard as she could to stay here with those she loved so dearly. She wanted to try every chemotherapy and treatment possible so that her family and friends would know how much she wanted to live.

She told me that she wished she had done more with her life and felt she didn't leave enough of a mark before her passing. I reminded her that she was giving all of us who know and love her, the greatest gift of all. She was teaching us that no one is guaranteed tomorrow. As her friends reach the mid-life point, and boy did it get here really fast, we are reminded that our spouses, children, families and friends are what truly matter in life. The energy we share between two human beings is what we get to take with us when we depart this planet. The house, the cars, and all of the stuff are left behind.

So, as the stress of everyday life creeps upon you, remember the gift that Kerry has given us. Be present in the moment, live your life to the *fullest. Laugh, love, and create memories with those you cherish.*

Yesterday's History
Tomorrow's a Mystery
Today is a Gift
That's Why We Call It the Present!
Thank you, Kerry, for sharing your life
with us. It is a gift we will all share.
We love you and will miss you, but you know.

Dr. Beth DuPree

5

Our Beloved Animals

When your heart centre opens in love
and kindness towards all creatures,
It begins to grow and expand as
light radiating forth . . .
By the power of this light, miracles can
be wrought, healings performed
And all the spiritual beauty of life is revealed.

WHITE EAGLE

Sheba

What the caterpillar calls the end of the world,
The master calls a butterfly.

Richard Bach

Tiger Puff, our calico cat, lived to the age of six-teen before dying from feline leukemia. Her death hit us hard; she had been in our family for many years and with me from elementary school through college. We were without a cat for nearly two years before a new ball of fur rolled into our lives.

Sheba came bounding into the room as a surprise from our parents. The long-haired kitten with glowing, yellow eyes and gray, white, and black fur immediately captured our hearts and filled the void left by Tiger Puff. As a kitten, Sheba was tiny—small enough to fit in the palm of my hand—and filled with enough energy to send her racing through the downstairs of the house and scurrying up the living room drapes. I can still hear my mom yelling out, "Sheba, get down!"

When she was young, Sheba had the most peculiar way of running; with her back arched, she'd run down the hall sideways. It was so cute and so funny. I wish I had a video or photo of her trick, which always surprised and delighted us.

The other thing I remember about Sheba was her love for Kentucky Fried Chicken. She picked up her taste for the Colonel from me; often, on my way home from work, I grabbed a box of chicken for dinner and often fed pieces to Sheba, even when she was a kitten. From then on, the only kind of chicken she would eat was KFC, and, of course, it had to be the Original recipe!

One night, just before bed, my dad turned on the automatic dishwasher. The machine cycled through, but the temperature control malfunctioned, and heating coils did not cool down. Sheba sensed something was wrong and jumped onto my parents' bed, meowing insistently. Finally, mom got up to investigate and found the countertop above the dishwasher blistering hot. Who knows what would have happened had our "watch cat" not been there to warn us?

When my parents moved to Lancaster County, two hours away, my relationship with Sheba soured. Mom offered that perhaps Sheba was upset because, in her view, I had left her. Over the next few years, Sheba became my mom's soul mate. When I visited, Sheba often was curled up on the bed in the master bedroom. She'd let me pet her, briefly, but within a few minutes, she would let out a hiss or whack me with her paw. And she had a mean right hook! At times she just scrambled off, seeking refuge under the bed. Our relationship became one of love and hate, with me often on the end of a mouthful of very sharp teeth. But despite the ornery behavior, I loved Sheba just as much as the first day she bounded into our lives.

When she was fourteen, Sheba stopped eating and lost weight. At Thanksgiving that year, she let me pet her more than usual; by Christmas she had died. I was heartbroken and put her photo by my computer.

Then one night, a few weeks after her passing, I had a vivid dream in which Sheba came to me. A bright light enveloped her as I held her in my arms one last time. I felt a warm rush through my body and a pure, encompassing love. For one brief moment I believe our souls intertwined. I knew she was saying, "I understand now. It's OK to let go." I awoke crying but felt refreshingly content.

I think of Sheba often, especially when passing a KFC. Occasionally, I'll stop and order an Original recipe and laugh as I picture Sheba running sideways down the hall or remember that tiny little ball of fur curled in my hands.

Jeff Werner

Little Peep

I have found that to love and be loved is the most empowering and exhilarating of all human emotions.

Jane Goodall

My little peep, dear little friend is my colorful little soul mate. A peachy-faced lovebird, Periwinkle Dreidel turned nineteen this September. She is not your ordinary specimen. She has a bright orange band surrounding her beak, sunshine yellow on the top of her head, shades of lime green and soft gray down her back, and a tail that flirts iridescent blue.

She is my little fighter, and when provoked or displeased, will peck at the red rubber toy suspended in her cage.

Our daughter, Corrine, chose her as a Hanukah gift in 1990. Our son, Ari, remarked, "I have known her all my life." Lately, she has become our third child.

Empty nesters, both our children live on the west coast. My husband, David, who for years covered his head, fearful that she would mistake it for a nest, has forged a close bond with her. Each morning he is the first to greet her, uncovering her cage as he waits for the coffee to perk.

Peri has a keen sense of smell and will begin to chirp in the morning the minute she hears us in the bedroom at the far end of the hall. At the end of the day, when we step off the elevator and walk toward the front door to our apartment, she is already greeting us. If she is feeling especially lonely, she refuses to let me out of her sight. On one occasion I took her with me into my meditation room so she would quiet down. After a few minutes she began to chirp quizzically, wondering why I was sitting so quietly by her side. That was the first and only time I brought her with me to meditate.

Very smart and creative for such a little bundle, Peri is an artist in her own right. During the year she will work on scraps of magazines that I leave at the bottom of her cage. She will cut out feathery strips with her beak or create small pieces of confetti. This habit is inherent in lovebirds and part of their nesting routine. Even when they no longer are laying eggs, they will continue to make art. I hope to use these precious scraps by designing a series of collages a la Matisse.

My little friend has always been here to cheer me up. She listens to my banter and most definitely picks up on my every mood. This year has been especially challenging. Our much loved farmhouse, "Bryn-tun" was sold and demolished by the new owners. The house originally was built in the 1800's and purchased by my grandparents in the 1940s. Many wonderful memories are associated with the house.

I also lost my father this past January. My dad loved Peri, and when he came to visit, as he walked in the door, headed straight to the kitchen to greet his friend. To lose him and the house in the same year was especially difficult for my brothers and me.

Shortly after my father died I noticed that Peri wasn't her exuberant self. She spent more time resting, had lost her appetite, and seemed more somber. A visit to the vet uncovered two esophageal tumors. The vet told us that she was a very sick bird and recommended we put her to sleep so that she wouldn't suffer.

On my way home I realized that Peri had felt my grief. I knew that during the past months she hadn't received much attention. I began to spend more time with her, enveloping her in a soft fleece, sending her Reiki, and reciting healing mantras as she rested.

In my journal I wrote:

I can't stand the thought
of losing my beloved
green blue orange yellow
feisty little bundle of energy
so much happiness you have given me
to greet me every morning
protest at night
when I would cover your cage
like a belligerent child

my sweet sweet little darling bird
how much I love you
and don't want you to suffer
I only need to make
a decision as to
when
is the right moment
not too late and not too soon—
you have been my inspiration
my muse
you have been a part of my soul
and I will set you free
it has been a wonderful full life
having you with me
a bond that that I will treasure
forever . . .
be sure to return
and be near me in spirit
for I will always hear your distinctive
elated cry
as you would on tiptoes
jumping up in joy cry out
make me laugh
so many times
my periwinkle dreidel
my love
help me to know when
it is time . . .

After writing this poem, I decided to research tumors and homeopathic remedies and found that maitake mushroom extract possibly reduce the size of tumors. I gave her two drops in her drinking water.

Maybe it was all my prayers asking that she be able to spend a little more time with us, but slowly her spirit began to recover. Although she isn't cured, she has moments of her old, feisty self. Lately, we have nicknamed her Houdini because she has taken to escaping from her cage by gently opening up one of the three front doors with her beak. She hasn't performed this trick since she was a young bird.

I am grateful each day for the gift of her friendship and love.

Jennifer Brinton Robkin

$\mathcal{L}$osing Shona

*The Law of Love is that you are Love
And that as you give Love to others,
You teach yourself what you are.*

Gerald Jampolsky, M.D.,
Love Is Letting Go of Fear

My heart went out to Carol as she sat in tears sharing with me the story of losing her beloved dog. Just three weeks before Carol's dear old friend and companion, Shona, a beautiful miniature collie, had died on Valentine's Day. Carol's heart was torn apart by this loss.

Although she had the loving support of her husband, Alan, Carol found the nights difficult to bear. She often woke at 2 a.m., and was unable to go back to sleep. She thought of how Shona, seventeen, had been confused and in distress in the final weeks of her life. Suffering from arthritis, Shona had difficulty maneuvering and lying down. That last night, when Shona was in bed with her, Carol knew that her collie's time had come.

How difficult this must have been for Carol. Shona had come to her as a very sick puppy with a bladder condition. Carol nursed Shona back to health and for almost seventeen years, the collie had been by her side twenty-four hours a day. Shona also had been a constant companion, protector, and loyal friend to Carol's mom and had been a source of great comfort for Carol when her mother died and when Carol sold her store. During their seventeen years together, Shona became a part of Carol's identity, and the loss of her collie threw Carol into confusion and pain.

Carol missed Shona's kisses, her presence, and her spirit, but in the weeks following Shona's death, Carol also realized that she needed this time without Shona to rediscover her own resources. She needed to heal, and to form a new identity, one that did not include her old friend and companion.

Loss pushes us to difficult places where we have not been before. We often question whether or not we have the courage and stamina to survive the pain. However, we often are given gifts that tell us that we are not alone and that we can withstand the journey.

Carol's first gift arrived a few days after Shona died. Carol was awakened at 4 a.m. by what felt like a swipe across her back. She recognized the swipe as the cuddling style of her first dog, Tiger and said to herself, "That was Tiger, for sure!" Carol knew that Tiger had come back to comfort her.

One morning Carol awakened from a dream in which she was in Africa with a man who cared for orphaned animals. In her dream an elephant and several cats were limping. While Carol was talking to the man, they heard a large crash and ran outside to discover a lion had been hit by a Federal Express truck backing up. Carol's heart broke for this young lion, because she knew that there would be no miracle healing. She realized that the lion in the dream was Shona, because the lion had a mane very similar to Shona's fur. And just as the vet had told Carol that nothing more could be done in the final moments of Shona's life, nothing could be done to save the lion. This dream, for Carol, was a sign that Shona was with her.

Shona found other ways to let Carol know she was with her. In the days following Shona's death, Carol was driving to a Reiki class and noticed a beautiful red-tailed hawk circling in the sky. After class, two more red-tailed hawks circled her car; by day's end Carol had seen five of these birds, and in the days following, Carol reported continued visits from Shona in the form of red-tailed hawks! This excited and touched Carol deeply. The hawks sometimes showed up in pairs, other times when Carol was leaving a store, or driving home, but always in places where Carol had not previously seen red-tailed hawks.

One weekend Carol was having a particularly difficult time, grieving deeply and crying. She and her husband, Alan, went out to sit on their porch and spotted three red-tailed hawks flying overhead. One of the hawks separated from the other two and descended, making a pass at Carol and Alan. For Carol, this was more than a sign, but an interaction. Even Alan felt stunned by what he had seen, and Carol was glad that he had been there to witness it. She described the hawk's action as having "raised" her up, and she knew this was the power of love. This incident was transformative for Carol; she felt her grief lift. Shona's visit and connection filled Carol with love and gave her a sense of peace.

In the weeks that followed, Carol improved in many ways. She had more energy, worked in her garden and signed up for an art class. With her study of Reiki, she also took time each day to meditate, to go to a deep place of truth within her being, enabling her to relax and shift her energy to a higher vibration. With her heart opening, she found a higher level of well-being and peace, attracting, similarly, new and meaningful experiences and synchronistic events.

She also met with an animal communicator and enjoyed wonderful moments connecting with her beloved collie. These moments were so powerful for Carol that she decided to study animal communication. As she continued to heal, she had a very special dream in which Shona appeared walking in the rain, something she had always disliked. But Shona appeared to have an invisible shield around her, as her fur was completely dry. She seemed healthy as though nothing was bothering her, not even her arthritis. Carol told me, in her dream:

I saw her and stopped. I did not call to her, and she didn't look at me, but we both knew the other was there. We were with each other but in a different way. I watched her go off, seeming very happy. It was special and truly healing—seeing her in such a good place, without pain or suffering. I felt such a sense of relief. I felt wonderful!

Shortly after the dream, Carol attended an art class that lasted an exhausting five hours. She surprised herself by making it through, realizing she had reclaimed the power she had lost with Shona's death. As she got into her car, she spotted several red-tailed hawks circling, and smiled, pleased they'd found her. The red-tailed hawks, she knew, were messengers, and Shona was responsible for this. Carol was deeply moved. "She has changed my life with her death. It is incredible that she has given me this gift." She continued, "I feel such a sense of gratitude, so very loved. Shona is now Spirit—and always with me."

Luca Brazzi

When you were born, you cried and the world rejoiced.
Live your life in such a manner that when you die
The world cries and you rejoice.

Old Indian Saying

After years of battling chronic fatigue syndrome, Ben Bishop felt that his life was about to take a turn for the better. His mother, Charlotte, reported that Ben was excited about the next stage in his life. Because he was doing so well, no one expected him to die.

He'd been diagnosed with chronic fatigue five years earlier. He continued to work through the first two years of his illness, but by the third year was so disabled that he was forced to go on disability.

His symptoms prohibited him from being as active as he once had been. His sister, MaryAnn, worried about his increasing sedentary lifestyle and the effect on his health. She encouraged Ben to get a puppy, and once he agreed, they traveled together to Harrisburg where he picked out an adorable, tiny, black pug.

What a difference this little puppy made in Ben's life! Named after a character in *The Godfather One,* Luca Brazzi was a furry ball of energy. Luca needed to be fed, walked several times a day, trained, played with, and taken to the vets for check-ups and shots. Ben was on the move with his new puppy.

Ben would hold Luca on his lap or in his arms, cradling him the way one would a baby. He took him into the pool and swam with him. Luca sustained Ben and helped him to heal. This is the power of our animals. They heal us with their love.

During the next two years Ben became stronger and healthier. He bought a home and was making plans to move in. On the night before settlement, he had a heart attack and died.

Sadly, it was his mom, Charlotte, who found him the next morning when she went to wake him before she left for work. When she saw that Ben was not responsive, she called 911 and tried to resuscitate him.

As the days and weeks passed, Charlotte noticed that Luca refused to go into Ben's room. He had always slept in Ben's bed, but when Charlotte called 911 and the paramedics had come to resuscitate Ben, Luca became frightened and ran from the room confused. Not only would Luca not go into the room, but he seemed very uncomfortable anywhere near it.

Charlotte, MaryAnn, and her two daughters, Amy and Amanda, believed that perhaps the energy of Ben's soul might still be present in the bedroom and seeking liberation. A friend recommended a ritual to cleanse the room, so that Luca might once again feel comfortable sleeping, curled, at the foot of Ben's bed.

These four women, representing three generations of women who deeply loved Ben, entered his room. One carried a vase filled with white roses; another carried a tall white candle; a third carried a prayer. They placed the vase on a table and the candle in the center of the room. Gathered in a circle, they prayed and asked that Ben's soul be freed, that the room be cleansed and blessed with healing and love.

Their eyes filling with tears, they finished their prayer. Suddenly, Luca dashed into the bedroom. He jumped up onto the edge of the bed, eyes sparkling, wagging his tail. Seeing him, Charlotte, MaryAnn, and her daughters knew that their prayer had been answered. In spite of their grief, they felt a profound joy—not only a loving connection to Ben, but the presence of a loving power that wished to honor their desire. In the midst of loss, their love, offered in prayer, provided them with a healing and hope.

For the next month, Luca seemed less anxious. His old habit of barking and chasing cars resumed. He even barked at the cars he saw on television.

One afternoon Luca was on the patio without a leash. MaryAnn went inside to get some papers, and Charlotte, who was on the phone, looked out the window to see the patio gate wide open. She heard Luca barking. Charlotte and MaryAnn ran out of the house to the street, but it was too late. Luca, who loved anything with wheels, had heard the mail truck coming down the street and had run out to chase it. He was hit by the wheels of the truck.

It was devastating for both mother and sister to lose this precious companion of Ben's. They missed Ben dearly. Charlotte told me what a gentle, caring soul he was. "He was such a handsome, well-mannered, young man," she said, "full of laughter and always there for me." In the way that Luca sustained Ben, he also sustained Charlotte and MaryAnn in their grief by providing them with an almost tangible sense of Ben's presence.

Weeks later a family member said to Charlotte, "I bet that Ben went to St. Peter and said, "Saint Peter, I would like my dog, please. Can you help me?"

Charlotte smiled as she told me this. "That brings me so much comfort." Despite the pain of losing her son and his dog, it pleased her to think that they were reunited again. Believing they were together eased her pain.

Our pets bring us great joy. They come into our lives to help us experience greater peace and bliss. As in Ben's case, they also help us to heal. Often, pets find a way to leave after their owners die. I wonder, don't you, how many of those who physically leave us, ask for the company of their little partners?

6

Intuition

Cease trying to work everything out with your mind.
It will get you nowhere.
Live by intuition and inspiration and
let your whole life be a revelation.

EILEEN CADDY

Mary's Signs

Meaning isn't what the situation gives us.
It's what we give the situation.

Marianne Williamson

On Christmas morning, I awoke feeling heavy hearted and thinking of my dad. This was the day, a year before, he had fallen and lost consciousness. He died four days later. The ring of the phone interrupted my thoughts. It was Mary, my father's caretaker, who had known and loved him as though he were a family member. She had worked for my dad since my mom's death, and her voice, for me, was a gift, as close to angels speaking as any voice could be.

We talked for awhile, Mary sharing with me several stories that confirmed what I had always known about her—which is that she is highly intuitive and has received throughout her life significant information through dreams. Let me explain:

After my mother's death, when Mary and I were cleaning out my parents' home, she told me that my mom had come to her in a dream, asking her to care for my dad.

She also told me that her Uncle Robert had died just a few days earlier. A few weeks before his death she'd had a dream that made her realize he was unlikely to live much longer.

In the dream she saw three visitors coming to her home. One was a child; the other two were an older man and woman. In the dream, the child ran off, the couple chasing after him. Mary recalled seeing the three of them running, disappearing into the mist. When she woke, Mary realized that she was being told that family members were coming to take her uncle, and that he soon would be transitioning. Knowing that her uncle would soon die, she made every effort to be with him each day in the days leading up to his death.

Mary had a second message about her uncle while at home alone. She had been thinking about her uncle in the hospital when she heard three knocks at the door. When she answered the door, no one was there. Mary knew, intuitively, that this was another way her loved ones were letting her know that something was about to happen to her uncle, an awareness that loved ones were preparing her for the event.

Mary also received a message when her nephew was about to die. She was at home sitting quietly when she heard her nickname, Mag, being called; she heard it called three different times. She knew this was extraordinary, and again, that she was about to lose a family member.

And from the time she was six years old, each time a loved one's death was imminent, Mary has heard spiritual or celestial singing in her head. It is unsettling because she has no control over it, but it is another sign of the extraordinary.

Love is a powerful force. There is nothing in this world, no other energy as powerful as the force of genuine, unconditional love. Mary represents this kind of love. Mary's experiences are grounded in the loving being that she is. Love does not die and continues to speak to us through dreams, knocks on the door, voices and songs.

The Visitor

The only real valuable thing is intuition.

Albert Einstein

We'd never met, but after reading *Touched by the Extraordinary*, Lisa called my office offering compliments and shared with me the following story.

She had lived in Yardley, Pennsylvania more than a decade before. Across the street from her house was a family, Ann, her husband, and their two sons, one of whom had leukemia. Lisa felt a deep and empathic connection with the family, and on her daily walks, she often found herself looking at their home, wondering how they were managing.

Sadly, the son died just before Passover. On the evening of the first Seder, while Lisa was out walking, she noticed a young man entering the house along with an elderly gentleman. The elderly man was portly and wearing a very crumpled suit. When Lisa saw Ann a few days later, she asked how the family was doing and mentioned the company they had for the Seder. Ann was stunned by Lisa's comment; not only had they not had any visitors, but Lisa's description of the older man was very familiar.

"That is my father, this person you describe!" Ann said with certainty. "He was born in France and died many years ago. How could you have known this? I have never told you about him."

Ann told Lisa that she had, in fact, felt the presence of others at the Seder table. Lisa's having seen the boy and the elderly man validated Ann's sense that her son and her father had been present to share the holiday with her. This touched and comforted her very much.

When Lisa related this story to me, she explained that when she feels a deep affection for others, she is able to receive what they need. Her intuition is rooted in a foundation of compassionate love.

We all are capable of knowing and sensing what Lisa experiences. It takes practice and the ability to relax; go into the silent stillness deep within you, stay present, fill your heart with love, and focus on the other being with the intention of receiving what you are able to on their behalf. Practice this, and before you know it, you, too, will be seeing with your mind's eye.

ℋ Listening Heart

At one level, intuition is a sixth sense.
At another, it is the "I" or the divinity
within which knows everything.
If the divinity within is sufficiently developed,
it is all conscious and knows all things.

White Eagle

Within each and every one of us is an inherent guidance system. We are not thrown helplessly into a seemingly cold and cruel world without the necessary tools for taking care of ourselves. Yet, most people go through an entire lifetime never realizing the power they have at their command. This power is not the exclusive province of gurus, avatars, or saints but is available to all people as their cosmic birthright.

The power lies within waiting to be tapped by anyone willing to use it. It is always there providing direction for our lives. But because we are surrounded by the noise and activities of everyday—outside existence—we tend to not hear the gentle prodding from within. We become blind and deaf to the sights and sounds of our higher selves. To begin using this guidance, one must first become aware of its existence and then trust in following its direction. My true life story is an excellent example of this principle.

My wife, Mardai, and I had been married for several years when we felt it was time to start raising a family. She asked, "Why not start with an adopted child?"

My wife and I both were of East Indian descent and decided to adopt a baby girl from India. We contacted the necessary agencies. There was an ocean of bureaucratic and political red tape, but the aura around us was one of excitement and anticipation. Finally, after seven months, only one document remained to be processed by the Immigration Department. Then something went wrong. We were informed that it would be another week or two before the necessary visa for our "soon to be" daughter would be issued. After months of waiting, another week seemed inconsequential, but that same day a telegram arrived from India telling us that a baby girl, a few weeks old, was available for adoption, and we should travel to Bombay as soon as possible to complete the formalities of the adoption process. This was the notice for which we had waited seven months. Everything was in order except for that one visa document. But in a week we would be on a plane, our first visit to India, and return home with our new baby daughter. All was well.

But all was not well. That night I could hardly sleep. My sleeplessness could have been attributed to my excitement and anticipation, but that was not so. Instead, there was an uneasy feeling within me, a strange premonition of disaster. I was filled with over-whelming apprehension.

The next day, the feeling of anxiety increased. I could find no reason to justify such uneasiness. Try as I did, it was impossible to dismiss my feelings. I felt compelled to leave for India within twenty-four hours. I told those close to me, and all advised that I wait until the final papers were processed. It would only be another week, they reasoned. I had waited so long; surely a few more days would not make much difference.

I even called my attorney to ask if he thought it was necessary to wait for the final papers. His response was a resounding, "Yes!" My business associates, too, tried to talk some sense into me. "Why, John?" asked one of the wiser ones. "Why the rush? I have never seen you like this before."

I could not explain the strange urgency I felt. In desperation I finally phoned the Immigration Department and requested to speak with the officer handling the case. "Please, can you speed up this process?" I implored.

"We are doing the best we can," was the reply.

"I would really like to leave for India tomorrow. When the visa is ready, will you please air mail it to me in Bombay? I will leave you my address. I'd be grateful for your help."

"We are sorry, but we cannot do that. You will have to wait until everything is in order."

"What will happen if I leave tomorrow?" I asked.

"There would be longer and more serious delays. We suggest you comply with our procedures and wait until the papers are ready. Thank you for calling. Goodbye."

Experience has taught me to trust my feelings even when I do not understand them. So I disregarded everyone's advice, called the airlines, and made reservations for a flight leaving the next day. When I told my wife what I had done, she, too, thought I had lost my mind. "Why not wait for another week?" she asked. "Everyone seems to think it would be best."

"You wait if you want to," I replied, "but I am going to India to get our daughter." Never before had I spoken to her in that tone of voice.

"But the papers and final approval?" she protested.

Finally, my wife reluctantly agreed to humor me. The following day found us hurtling across the Atlantic on a 747 jet, the first leg of our journey to the mystical land of India. Exhaustion forced me into a deep sleep. When I awoke, we were somewhere over the continent of Africa. I was surprised that my feelings of doom and despair had vanished. I reflected on my behavior of the past day, but I did not regret my actions. It was almost midnight when we touched down at the International Airport in Bombay. What a joy it would be to see our daughter the next day.

First thing in the morning we were off to the agency. We introduced ourselves to the manager and waited anxiously while they went off for the baby girl who was to be our daughter. There are times when seconds seem like hours, and this was one such time. Finally a nurse arrived carrying a little bundle. As we looked at the baby wrapped in the bundle, a sense of shock overcame us. Our child, whom we had imagined as a healthy six or seven pound baby, was an emaciated little thing, weighing slightly more than three pounds. She was suffering from malnutrition and was covered with sores. Only her eyes moved as they followed us around the room. "This baby is very sick," said the nurse. "The doctor thinks that she might not live through the day. Would you like to consider taking another child?"

Anger, resentment, and fear sprung up within me. After all the preparation and hope, to finally be faced with the possibility of losing the child was unthinkable. No! We had not gone through everything for this. Something had guided me, against the dictates of reason, to be where I was at that moment. The infant must not die. Now I understood why I felt compelled to leave for India when I did. A day or two later and the child surely would have died. By being in India, I was able to do whatever was possible to save her life. "No!" I fairly shouted. "We'll take our baby. This way she has at least one chance in a thousand. Leaving her here, she has none."

Without hesitation we asked for the necessary documents and signed them. Quickly we left with the little bundle in our arms. We went directly to the office of a pediatrician whom friends back in the United States had recommended. While examining the child, the pediatrician asked, "Do you know what you have done? This child is deathly ill. I don't know if she'll make it." The desperation in my heart was being replaced by a strong determination and a sense of purpose. Almost in tears I looked at the doctor and pleaded, "Please do all that you can."

It was impossible to get the child into the hospital because of local laws and customs. With the help of the good doctor we were able to obtain the services of an additional doctor and two nurses. Fortune smiled on us, for one of the nurses was a woman who once attended to Mahatma Gandhi. She was full of compassion and competency and understood our plight. That night, in a hotel suite overlooking the Arabian Sea, the nurses and doctors worked feverishly to keep our child alive. We made it through the night.

Days ran into weeks, and our daughter gradually improved, though she was far from being out of danger. Because I had left the United States without the proper visa papers, the red tape compounded itself. We were informed by the American Embassy in Bombay that a new application for a visa had to be filled out and sent in for approval. In the meantime, rumor had it that the Indian Government was about to declare emergency rule. There was unrest in the street.

As if we didn't have enough to worry about, we were displaced from our hotel to make room for some wealthy, visiting Arabs. We found new lodging in a small, rundown hotel. Money was running short, our child's life was still in danger, and other problems seemed overwhelming.

Back in the United States, some friends and influential business associates had heard of our plight and had petitioned our government leaders to do something about it. However, we could not wait. We had to take the baby back to the United States for proper medical care. Without a visa for our child, it was impossible for us to get her on a plane, and even if we did, there would be other difficulties with the Immigration Department when we arrived home. Yet, where there is a will, there is a way. Somehow, with the help of a few Indian friends and the guidance of my inner voice, we managed to pass through several checkpoints at the airport in Bombay and literally "smuggled" our child aboard a plane bound for the United States. Finally, we were on our way home.

Arriving in New York after a long and tiring flight, we were apprehensive that the Immigration Department would deport our daughter for lack of a visa. Again, fortune smiled on us. There was no need to worry. Our friends had prevailed on our government to make an exception, and we were welcomed home by a delegation. A visa was issued on the spot.

We named our daughter Malika. With proper medical care she continued to make progress. Today, she is a happy, healthy young woman with a degree in Business Administration from a university nearby. She remembers very little of her early years. But when I look into her beautiful dark eyes, I relive the steps that brought her to us. Had I not followed the strange feelings of urgency to leave for India on that day many, many years ago, my daughter would not be here today.

John Harricharan

The Ninety-third Caller

*The distance between Life and Death
may not be as great as you think.*

Morrie Schwartz

The years following Mardai's death were especially
difficult as John worked to feed and care for his
children, as well as to pay off the medical bills that had
accumulated during Mardai's illness.

When Malika was a senior in high school, John
bought her an old car. Unfortunately, when she took
the car in for a check-up, she was told that it would
cost eight hundred dollars to fix. John, at that time,
simply didn't have the money.

But a few days later, while she was doing her home-
work, Malika felt an intuitive urge to turn on her radio.
She heard an announcement that invited listeners to call
in. "Dial this number, and if you are the ninety-third

caller, you will win the prize." She called in, but the line was busy, and she hung up. A while later, and again feeling an intuitive urge, she called back, and this time got through. Yes, she was the ninety-third caller, and had won one thousand dollars! Later she told her father, "Mommy told me to call and to call again."

Malika had enough money not only for the repairs to the car, but she also had another two hundred dollars left for herself. She had listened to her intuitive knowing, and she knew that her mom continued to guide and care for her. She knew she was not alone.

Rose Quartz Heart

Now I know that cold steel
is not what heals,
but the love and warmth that emanates sincerely
from my heart.
This awareness required a shift
in my consciousness and a greater awareness
of the human being I am treating.

Beth DuPree, M.D.,
The Healing Consciousness

Little did Sharon know that she would follow her own cancer journey. Eight years after her mom died, Sharon was diagnosed with breast cancer. Prior to her diagnosis, Sharon experienced an overwhelming sense that there was cancer in her body. For years she struggled with a number of stressful situations, and she knew that the stress was taking a toll. Her health problems were beginning to accumulate.

She had been on leave from work due to injuries from a fall. The injury resulted in a herniated disk in her back and swollen legs. She also severely traumatized her breast and sustained a bruise the size of a grapefruit. As a wife and mom to three teenage daughters, it was inconvenient to stay at home recuperating, but Sharon took advantage of the time and scheduled her annual mammogram.

Almost a year to the day from her previous mammogram, Sharon went into the office for what should have been a routine appointment. It was anything but. The mammogram revealed something suspicious in the right breast, and Sharon was asked to return for a second set of images. After the second mammogram, the radiologist called Sharon in to her office to tell her that there was an area of concern. She recommended a stereotactic core biopsy.

Wasting not a moment, Sharon scheduled the biopsy for the following week. The result confirmed a diagnosis of breast cancer.

Her family and friends were quick to offer their support, sending cards and small gifts to cheer her. Among the gifts was a small box with a note, *Eric gave this to me when I needed a little hope and optimism in my life. I hope it brings you the same comfort and joy that it brought to me. Love you!* Inside the box, nestled in layers of pink netting, was a pink quartz heart. Eric was a close friend and fellow teacher who had battled cancer and died just a few months earlier. "The pink heart became a symbol of the overflowing generosity of all those who supported and cared for me," said Sharon.

At her doctor's recommendation, Sharon scheduled a lumpectomy. She considered obtaining a second opinion, and several friends recommended Dr. Beth DuPree. Sharon began the process of having her records and specimen slides sent to the hospital where Dr. DuPree was on staff, but ultimately, she decided to forego a second opinion. She kept her surgery date for the lumpectomy with her original doctor.

After the surgery her doctor assured her that he had taken out a five centimeter mass and felt confident that all the cancer had been removed. "But when I looked at the results, I noticed there were four margins to pass," Sharon said, "and I had passed only one. Furthermore, the results of the MRI I'd had the week before had not been evaluated by the surgeon. He was unaware that there was a second tumor and two nodules in the breast."

The same week as her surgery, Sharon's husband was speaking to a co-worker who told him that his wife, an operating room nurse, worked with Dr. DuPree. He offered to have Sharon call his home to speak to his wife. Sharon listened carefully to the nurse and felt that she was being led to where she needed to go. She called Dr. DuPree's office to schedule an appointment.

As she drove to the doctor's office, she threw the small rose quartz heart into her purse. She told me, "Something made me take it with me. It served as a source of calmness for me."

While she and Dr. DuPree were chatting, Sharon explained that she worked at a local school.

Dr. DuPree's son attended the same school, and Dr. DuPree spoke of her son's fondness for his teacher, Eric, who recently had passed away. Sharon reached into her handbag, digging deeply to the bottom where the heart had fallen. When she showed the heart to Dr. DuPree, the doctor's eyes welled up with tears; it was the same heart she gives to all her patients who are diagnosed with cancer. "And here I was, carrying the same heart with me, compliments of Eric!" exclaimed Sharon. The two women knew, in that moment, that Eric had played a significant role in bringing Sharon to Dr. DuPree.

Following her exam, Sharon accompanied the doctor to her office where they sat side by side on the couch. Dr. DuPree recommended bilateral mastectomies. While she was explaining her reasons for the mastectomies, Sharon felt "this surge of energy that came from her and entered my body, settling in my core. I experienced a profound, positive energy that truly comforted me. I knew that Dr. DuPree was the breast surgeon I was meant to have in my life."

In Sharon's words, "I believe that God had a hand in the synchronicities that occurred. Because of Dr. DuPree, I learned that cancer also had developed in the ducts of the non-cancer breast. Although it had not shown up in the mammogram, the MRI or the PET scan, the pathology was evident in the tissue from the bilateral mastectomies."

For Sharon, cancer has been a powerful teacher. After the death of her mother, she experienced a moment when she heard God speak to her, "This is your life. Take this opportunity to listen and trust. I am here, and you are loved. Listen and trust." She felt deeply grateful for this message, embraced in a warm blanket of serenity. From that moment forward, she listened more carefully to her intuition. Cancer helped her to increase her awareness, and she has grown and experienced healing in all realms of her life.

"I was destined to explore the physical, emotional, and spiritual realms in my life. I truly was able to trust this doctor, and I will always be grateful for her presence in my life. The experiences that I have had and the lessons I have learned will be ones that I will take with me forever."

"God has blessed me with an abundance of gifts," Sharon explained. "His presence has made all the difference when facing adversity in my life. I have become a better listener to the messages meant for me, and I believe that the Universe conspires on my behalf all the time."

Finally Sharon stated, "I need to remind myself to stay tuned in, to give thanks often, and to share my love with others. I don't ever have to look very far to find God, if I remember to look within myself!"

7

Signs

Spiritual experience is not taught;
it is found, uncovered, discovered, and recovered.
These sorts of experiences are common.
They happen to all of us when least expected.
Many people discount them . . .
Yet, they can change our lives.

RACHEL NAOMI REMEN, M.D.,
My Grandfather's Blessings

Butterflies

Perhaps because the butterfly
Has already traveled the path of the man,
She sees his journey
Through the eyes of her heart and her soul.

Heather O'Hara,
Axis, The Song in the Center of the Soul

When a loved one dies, our hearts feel as those they have been broken in a million pieces. Often in our grieving and longing for our loved one, we ask for a sign, an indication that they are still with us in some way. Signs have the power to bring comfort and to heal the mind, body, and spirit. They do not take away grief, but they do soothe us when we are in pain. They also offer us the gift of hope—hope in an eternal life, hope that when we die our love will continue to live on.

One of my favorite stories from *Touched by the Extraordinary*, is of a family in which the father, a physician died. As Father's Day approached, his wife and children planned a special outing. While they were enjoying a picnic lunch, a butterfly appeared and hovered closely, floating from one family member to the next. The mom excused herself to go to the ladies' room, and when she returned was delighted to see the butterfly still there and resting right on top of a hamburger. Her children were all laughing. Their father had loved hamburgers, and seeing the butterfly resting on the hamburger was a sign to them that their dad was right there with them.

Recognizing signs helps us to develop our intuitive wisdom. After her daughter's death, Kim Wencl, whose story, "The Letter" appears in Chapter 1, learned to listen to the small, still voice inside. For Kim, the voice is the presence of her daughter, Liz. Kim's faith and connection to God help her to be more aware of and open to signs from Liz. She recently told me that Liz's close friend, Kira, had become engaged.

Late one afternoon Kira, and her boyfriend went for a walk. As they were talking, a lone butterfly flitted in and around their shoulders. Kira thought of Liz, and as the butterfly was fluttering close by, Kira's boyfriend dropped to his knees and proposed. Kira realized that the butterfly was Liz's way of communicating her presence and congratulations on her friend's engagement. When Kira later told Kim this story, Kim was touched and pleased to know that Kira had acted intuitively and was able to receive signs from Liz. Kim also believes that Liz is happy that her friends and loved ones are able to feel her presence.

Many patients have shared stories with me about butterflies hovering closely, following the death of a loved one. Scientifically, we know that everything is energy. With the death of a body, the energy is released and can merge into an animal, an insect, a bird, and can play havoc with anything that is dependent on electrical energy. Whether the sign arrives in the form of a bird, music, blinking lights, ladybugs, a feather, dreams, or a penny, it connects us powerfully to our loved one and reassures us that we are cared for.

Rainbows and Willie Nelson

*Love, that thing we have difficulty describing, is the
only truly real and lasting experience of life . . .
It is the source of happiness, the energy that
connects us and that lives within us.*

**Elisabeth Kubler-Ross, M.D.,
and David Kessler,** *Life Lessons*

Signs allow us to connect with our loved ones,
our angels or Source. When I visit my brothers
in Arizona, I always ask my mom and dad for a sign
that they are with us. Often I am given the sign of a
rainbow.

In fact, recently, during my nephew's graduation,
while we were waiting for the procession, the sky suddenly became quite dark and ominous. The wind picked
up, gusting, and it looked as though it was going to
pour rain. But there was a beautiful light shining over
the school, and as I looked to my right, I noticed the
beginnings of a small rainbow. I smiled, knowing that
my folks were giving me a sign that they were with us.

Synchronicities are a type of sign. A young woman I spoke with at a book signing told me a wonderful story of synchronicity involving rainbows. On the anniversary of a loved one's death, she and her brother were talking on the phone. As she was talking, she looked out the window and noticed a full rainbow had formed. She told her brother, and was stunned to hear him then describe the magnificent rainbow over his backyard, so large that he was able to see each of the colors and where the rainbow began and ended. They each realized in that moment that they were connecting to something extraordinary—their loved one.

Another friend also told me a story of synchronicity that took place right after she learned her mother had died. Val had a Christmas playlist on her computer and was playing Christmas carols when she received a phone call telling her that her mom had just died. When she hung up the phone, she noticed that the Christmas playlist was still highlighted, but a Willie Nelson song, not on the playlist, was playing. The Willie Nelson song had always had particular meaning to her family and was a favorite at her father's birthday dinners. Her brother and daughter, the technology experts, were baffled and unable to figure out what had happened. But for all of them it was a gift. In Val's words, "The emotional cord struck in hearing that song was deep."

Squirrels and Frogs

*It is only with the heart one sees rightly
that which is invisible to the eye.*

Antoine de Saint Exupery
The Little Prince

Since the death of her daughter, Elena has become so much more connected to the animal world. She explained, "I can almost feel and sense what Allie felt with these animals when she picked up a little lizard or an ant; it seemed that she could communicate and connect with them."

In the week following Allie's death, the house was filled with family and friends who were there to help and to offer support. Bob was making coffee in the kitchen when he noticed a squirrel at the glass kitchen door. It sat there staring in. This seemed rather odd, but he remembered what Elena had told him about Allie Bird, the Northern Mockingbird who had been visiting since the morning after Allie died. Bob ran to tell Elena, who was in the bathroom, taking a shower. "Get out," he said. "You have to come right now or you will miss it!"

And so, Elena, still wet, threw a towel around her and trudged through the hall, soaking the hardwood floors, guests still asleep upstairs. Bob urged, "Come on, come on! You've got to see this!" Sure enough, the squirrel was still there, staring quietly into the house through the glass door. The squirrel didn't move until Elena was two feet from the door, then it turned, suddenly, and ran away.

During the next year the squirrel visited them many times. Elena said, "I could go right up to the door and put my face up against the glass, and that squirrel just looked in and stared right at me. I wanted to get as close to it as I could." My husband laughed at me, because I crawled on the floor trying to get as close to the door as I could. Then, as I realized that this squirrel wasn't going anywhere, I found I could get a foot away from it, with just the glass between us. I remember, once, opening the door and Bob warning, 'Elena, you don't want that squirrel in the house!' Yes, I do, I thought."

Elena continued, "I had no fear of the squirrel. I wasn't afraid that it would run all over the house, tearing things up. I think that if it had come into the house, it might have let me pet it. Being close to that squirrel was my way of being near Allie. And, to this day, that is all I want."

"Whether she is coming to say hello as a bird or a squirrel, I feel like Allie is saying, 'Mom, look at me!

I've got Harry Potter powers! Look at what I can do now! One day I can be a squirrel and the next day I can be a bird . . . and I can do all these things.'"

Elena continued, "I think when Allie comes to say hi and to visit with us, she also is letting us know that she is okay. I believe that we are communicating, heart to heart, mind to mind. Her signs are gifts to me, and I always say, 'Thanks for the hug,' or 'Thanks for the love' or 'Thanks for the little bit of confidence.'" Elena emphasized how very, very important it is to her to express her appreciation to Allie for giving her a sign.

Elena also told me how much Allie adored frogs. If a frog became stranded in the pool, Allie jumped in to rescue it.

A month after Allie's death, a frog was in the pool. Elena thought, "Oh, my God, she doesn't really expect me to go in the pool to rescue this frog, does she?"

"We took the skimmer and pulled the frog out of the pool. Kate, Allie's sister, reached into the skimmer to grab the frog. She had the frog in her open hand, palm face-up, with her fingers outstretched. The frog just sat quietly on her hand. She brought it over to Bob and me. We were all looking at the frog, and I said, 'Isn't it odd that this frog isn't jumping?'"

"Well, this frog did not go anywhere! We even brought it to Grandma for her to see it. The frog sat in Kate's hand for fifteen minutes, not hopping or wriggling to get away. Then, remembering that Allie had made a ceramic frog house in pottery class, we put the frog in Allie's frog house." Suddenly the frog hopped around. They now keep Allie's frog house in their garden.

Elena knows that Allie is using her energy and her love of animals to find ways to be present for her mom and her family. The energy of love is the energy of eternity. Love does not die and neither does energy. Allie finds ways to gently enter the lives of her loved ones, saying "Hi. I am here." For this, her mother is eternally grateful.

$\mathcal{A}$ Musical Bark

*Miracles and the meaningful coincidences of
our lives are evidence of our immortality.
They prove that we are "soul" and not just "stuff."*

Paul Pearsall, *Miracle in Maui*

Allie loved animals, and typical of most nine-year-olds, had a huge collection of stuffed animals. The day after her funeral, her mom, Elena, piled all of them in the corner of the playroom, and later in the evening, the family ended up in there sitting around telling wonderful feel-good Allie stories (see page 38).

Elena wanted each of Allie's friends and family members to choose one of Allie's stuffed animals to keep. While they were sharing stories, one of the animals in the pile suddenly began to bark! Everyone stopped talking and looked at one another. Then they got up and went over to the pile, looking through it to discover that the bark was coming from a stuffed, white poodle. Elena turned the switch to off and placed the poodle back in the pile, but a minute later, it began to bark again, so Elena picked it back up and held it.

While she was holding it, another dog began to bark. This one, a little, brown, stuffed dog that was voice-activated. The dog not only barked but also walked and rolled over when activated. The problem was that no one was wearing the microphone into which someone spoke to give instructions to the stuffed toy.

Allie's Uncle Bill was sitting on the futon watching. Allie dearly loved her Uncle, and as he was watching, the little brown dog walked right over to him barking. It sat at his feet, then stood again and continued to bark. Uncle Bill was a bit unnerved, so Elena pulled the dog back into the center of the room. And what do you think the little dog did? Yes, it walked right back to Uncle Bill.

Uncle Bill then got up and moved to the other side of the room, and immediately the little barking dog did a forty-five degree turn and followed him. Someone shouted, "Bill, Allie wants you to have that stuffed animal!"

The next morning Elena had the thought that perhaps Allie was trying to show them all how powerful she was. She said aloud, "Oh, my gosh, Allie is saying, 'Look at me! Look what I can do! Look at my Harry Potter magic!'"

She went into the playroom, brought out the stuffed dog and gave it a command to walk. The dog started to walk, and then stopped. As Elena moved away, the little dog started again, following her. For Elena, it was Allie saying, "No, I'm not going to walk when you say for me to; I'm going to do it on my own terms."

Uncle Bill stayed for several more days. One morning Elena got up early. The house was extremely quiet, and as she walked past the playroom where Uncle Bill was sleeping, she saw him through a crack in the door. He was sitting on the futon turning the little brown dog over and over, examining it.

He brought the stuffed toy into the kitchen, placed it on the counter and continued to fidget with it, trying to get it to bark or walk. Elena knew that the dog's antics from a few days before were driving him crazy. He could not figure out what had activated the little brown dog. For the rest of his stay, he continued to play with it, but nothing happened.

On the day he was leaving. Elena asked Uncle Bill if he had packed the dog. He replied that he was not planning to take it with him, and she said, "You are not leaving it here! Allie doesn't want it here; she wants it at your house. You have to take it with you." And with that Uncle Bill packed the dog in his bag.

As she said goodbye to Uncle Bill, Elena realized that in order for him to get the dog to bark, he needed to talk to and communicate with Allie. "Allie will not give you a sign unless you ask for it," she said.

Elena chose for herself the little, white poodle. She keeps it on the dresser in her bedroom. Several times, while quietly reading a book, the dog will bark unexpectedly, and she knows it is Allie's way of saying, "Hi, Mom! I'm here with you."

The Piano

The most beautiful thing we can experience is the mysterious.

Albert Einstein

John Harricharan told me that when his beloved, Mardai, died, he was uncertain how he would ever be able to care for their two children, Malika and Jonathan.

Years later, on August 14th, he, Malika and Jonathan were gathered together having dinner. They were celebrating Mardai's birthday and reminiscing when, suddenly, they heard piano notes being played. Mardai had been an exceptional pianist and had won several awards during her lifetime. But neither John nor his children played. In fact, since Mardai's death, no one had even opened the piano. John thought perhaps it was the cat walking across the keys, but when he turned, he spotted the cat sitting right next to him.

John decided he had imagined it when Malika abruptly blurted, "Dad, did you hear that?"

"Oh, it's just Mommy telling us that she is enjoying her birthday," said Jonathan matter-of-factly. "Mommy talks to me every day when I am getting off the bus in the afternoon and coming into the house." He told his Dad and his sister how his mom was always there to help him.

How wonderful for this family to know that their wife and mom was right there with them as they were celebrating her birthday and their life together.

My Heart Will Go On

*Every time a heart cracks . . . somewhere,
something beautiful is being born.*

Oprah Winfrey

According to Natalie Kaye (see page 59), the night her mom was taken to the ICU was a terrible night. Earlier in the evening she had spiked a fever and was deteriorating rapidly. The family needed help and knew that their mom needed to be hospitalized. That night no one slept.

But that same evening, on the hospital television, there was a showing of the movie *The Titanic*. Even now Natalie associates that evening and her mom with the music. What especially moves her are the words of the song, "My Heart Will Go On."

It is these words that Natalie hears on anniversaries and special occasions. A few years ago, on her birthday, she and a friend were shopping in New Hope, Pennsylvania. As they walked into a store, Natalie heard the music and the words, "my heart will go on." She was stunned and felt her heart race, wondering if she was imagining hearing the song. She turned to her friend, "Do you hear that song?" "Yes," her friend replied. "That's the theme from *The Titanic*." Natalie smiled, delighted. She knew her mother was right there with her, wishing her a beautiful birthday.

Over the years, Natalie has often heard this music around the time of her birthday. She has come to know that it is her mom speaking to her and sharing in her celebrations. What a special gift!

The Cyclamen

*In the depths of my deepest winter,
I finally learned that within me
there lay an invincible summer.*

Camus

Natalie lost her entire immediate family within three years (see pages 59, 152). Her father died in 1994 and her sister the following year in 1995. In 1996 her mom died. She told me, "I was so broken down I could not function. I had lost three family members, and I needed three years to fully grieve for them."

Shortly after her mom's death, Natalie moved into her new home. A good friend gave her a beautiful cyclamen plant as a house warming gift. Cyclamens were one of her mom's favorite plants. Natalie placed it on a stand near the dining room table.

Cyclamens generally live for six months. But much to Natalie's surprise and delight, hers lived for three years. Natalie believed that her plant's long life and constant blooming was because her mom wished to stay close to her.

Natalie also realized during this time that she hadn't fully grieved for her father and sister. Because of illnesses, their deaths were not unexpected, and Natalie returned to work without allowing herself to mourn her losses. Her mom's death, however, was sudden, and the shock of it triggered a deep grief for all three loved ones. "I needed to grieve for all three of them. And this took three years, the length of the life of my cyclamen plant!"

The cyclamen helped Natalie heal. In Natalie's words, "There are ways our loved ones talk to us. Life is eternal. People need to know this, because it is so very comforting."

$\mathcal{A}$ Breeze, a Gust of Wind

The soul is not an idea or a belief; it is an experience.
It may awaken in us through dreams,
music, art or work or parenthood . . .
or sometimes for no reason at all.

Rachel Naomi Remen, M.D.,
My Grandfather's Blessings

Natalie's sister, Rhoda, waged a valiant battle with breast cancer for more than seven years. She died just before her forty-ninth birthday, on Friday, March 18th, 1995. Rhoda was to be buried in California, where she had lived, on the following Monday, the first day of spring (see page 154).

Natalie traveled to California for the funeral, arriving before other family members. It was a difficult trip, and she was filled with enormous grief. She felt strange and lonely being alone in the house without her sister. The day before the funeral, Natalie was resting in the bedroom where she usually stayed when visiting her sister. Overwhelmed with grief, she could not stop crying.

Suddenly, she heard a voice within her, her sister, Rhoda's voice. The voice spoke clearly, "Do not be sad, sister. I have not left you. I'll never leave you. I am One with everything. Look for me in the wind."

"I didn't know what Rhoda meant," said Natalie, "but I soon understood her words." At the cemetery on Monday, as the casket was being lowered into the ground, entering the earth, a strong wind gusted. "It just came out of nowhere," said Natalie. "Everything seemed to be flapping in the wind!"

Since then, every time Natalie thinks of her sister, a breeze stirs. "I feel it is God and my sister speaking to me," said Natalie. "I feel grateful and so connected to them."

8

Angels

And the angel said,
"I have learned that every man lives
not through care of himself,
but by love.

LEO TOLSTOY

Susan's Angels

*You don't need a formal prayer or invocation
to call the Angels to your side.
Simply think, "Angels, please surround
me," and they are there.*

Doreen Virtue, Ph.D, *Divine Guidance*

Hope comes in many forms, but one of our greatest sources of hope and inspiration appears in the form of angels. Angels are ever present, and each of us has at least one. In fact, in a recent poll, 69% of the public indicated a belief in angels. And doesn't it astonish us when we are given the gift of evidence that our angels are listening to us? I was blessed to have such a moment several years ago.

On a damp, cloudy day in March 2004, while sitting at my computer working to finish the final version of *Touched by the Extraordinary*, I had a sudden feeling that something was very wrong downstairs. As I ran to the top of the staircase, I heard water, too much water, gushing out of my washing machine. I ran down the steps into the kitchen. My heart felt as though it had sunk to my feet. There was water everywhere! Not just a little, but several inches filling my laundry room and kitchen. Even worse, I could hear water dripping into my basement. I opened the basement door and ran downstairs only to find water from the overhead pipes flooding our pool table, exercise equipment, and boxes filled with my husband's office files. I was completely overwhelmed—and totally alone in the house.

After moving the files to safer ground, I retrieved the water vacuum, only to find it was full of water and very heavy. I dragged it over to the sump pump in the corner of the basement to empty it, water spilling from the pipes, flooding the basement. Once emptied, I hauled the vacuum up the stairs to clear the water from the first floor, huffing and puffing my way through this, knowing that I was in a race against time. The faster I worked, the more I might be able to minimize the damage. Once I had vacuumed up most of the water, I dragged the machine back down to the basement to empty and began to suck up the water there. My adrenalin was working full force, pushing me, giving me the strength to do the impossible. But little by little, after several more trips to empty the vacuum, and after clearing most of the water from both floors, I felt myself wearing out.

I crawled upstairs to my bedroom, sat on the edge of my bed, and burst into tears, exhausted.

I remember clearly pleading, "Please, please, angels help me! I need help!" I was worn out and exhausted.

Then the phone rang! It was my husband calling to tell me that I had a patient in my office who insisted on seeing me; she had a package she wanted to give to me. I didn't see how I could leave the house at this time, but something in my husband's voice convinced me to throw on my coat and head to my office, ten minutes from home.

Minutes later, as I opened my office door, I was stunned to see Anna, a patient with whom I had been working for several months. In one hand she was carrying a woven wooden basket in which she'd packed a container of soup, a sandwich, and a small vase brimming with newly budded daffodils. In her other hand was a large, heavy, wrapped package. I hugged her, thanking her for her kindness, and told her about my flooded house. With compassion and understanding, she reminded me that there were others who were dealing with situations far more difficult than my own. Her words were precisely what I needed to hear at that moment, and I knew that she came from a place of knowing, having lost, in a very short time, her son, her sister, her mother, and the therapist who had been supporting her through her losses. Her wisdom and the gifts that she brought for me, clearly, were sent to me by my angels.

But there was more. After thanking her from the depths of my heart for these exquisite gifts for my soul, we said goodbye. After she left I put the large, heavy brown paper package she had given me on the floor and took a peek to see what it was. To my amazement, it was the most precious, unique angel I could have been given. I filled with tears of gratitude. My angels, indeed, had heard me.

I felt light, better, and more hopeful when I returned home to my water soaked kitchen and basement. I called the insurance adjuster, and within the hour, help arrived. Huge fans were installed throughout the basement and first floor, and I was assured that we would have insurance coverage for our losses.

The most wonderful memory of that afternoon, however, was the basket of fragrant yellow daffodils that brought me peace and joy every time I gazed at them. They and the delicious soup and sandwich were sustenance for my soul. Yes, my angel had found a way to care for me so like the warm embrace my mom would have given me had she been there to help. I felt cared for, blessed, and watched over by God and the Universe.

I have been blessed by those I cannot see, but whose presence I feel. I know that I am not alone and hope that you, too, will find that, even in the most difficult situations, you are fully supported by the universe. All that is required is that you ask for help. It is there waiting for you.

A Russian Angel

*Your two guardian angels are always with you.
The other angels come and go as we need them.*

Doreen Virtue, Ph.D., *Divine Guidance*

Janie Hermann, a librarian, and her husband, were traveling for the second time to Saint Petersburg, Russia to meet and bring home their new baby son. The trip did not go well; because of changes in the law, the court hearing for the adoption had been canceled. They extended their visit, hoping to appeal the new law, but their requests were declined. And because they stayed longer than anticipated, they had to rebook their flight home; the first available flight was a 6:45 a.m. flight.

In Janie's own words:

We were emotionally exhausted and distraught. We felt like we were in a nightmare without escape, running on adrenalin as we made our way to the airport. It was 5:00 a.m. in the St Petersburg airport, and though we had our one-way tickets waiting for us at the Air France check-in, the security guard would not let us through the gate to get them. She did not speak English well, and we did not speak Russian well enough to explain that we couldn't show her our tickets because they were being held at the Air France desk.

She sent us on a wild goose chase to the Air France office two buildings away. It was still dark out and raining. I was soaked and exhausted by the time I got to the office, only to find that they didn't open until 7:00 a.m. Our flight was scheduled to leave at 6:45 a.m.

I no longer had any strength left. I sat down outside the office and started to sob. It was our third wedding anniversary, and we were supposed to be bonding with our new son.

Instead I was locked out of the Air France office while my husband stayed back at the terminal with our luggage.

Out of nowhere came a large, Russian business man who also had been given a hard time by the security guard and sent to the Air France office. He saw me crying and asked what was wrong. In great, gulping sobs, I told him my story, and he said simply, "Follow me."

I ran to keep up with him as he went to the airport terminal to talk to the security guard.

The two of them began gesturing and shouting at one another, but after what seemed like an eternity, but was probably only a minute or two, he said, "You are cleared. Go get your tickets."

I left to get my husband, but when I got back the man was gone. We looked for him in the crowd, but he disappeared without us having a chance to properly thank him. Had it not been for him, we would have been stuck in Russia with expiring visas and no tickets home.

Janie prefaced this story by telling me, that as a result of these events, she absolutely knows we have angels caring for us.

Janie Hermann

An Angelic Stranger

*I saw them with my bodily eyes as clearly as I see you.
And when they departed, I used to weep and
wish they would take me with them.*

Saint Joan of Arc

My friend, Rosalie, deeply grieved the souls who were lost on September 11th, 2001. Many were friends and members of our Bucks County community. Watching the rescue efforts and hearing the daily news reports on television were heartbreaking for her. The last thing she felt like doing was going with her husband, Lou, to a billiards competition in Chesapeake, Virginia, but because Lou wanted to go, she felt she should go with him.

The tournament was held in a large gymnasium. Rosalie sat in the back, unable to focus on the competition. Her thoughts kept returning to the events of 9/11, and she found herself praying both for those who had died and those who were grieving their loved ones.

As Rosalie was sitting quietly, a young man sat down in the empty seat beside her. They began talking. Rosalie had a vague sense of the man's size and build. He seemed to be in his mid-thirties, fair-complexioned, and wearing brown trousers and a shirt, but later she could not recall his face.

They talked. He seemed to sense Rosalie's sadness and pain. Looking directly into her eyes, he told her to pray for the souls she grieved, reassuring her that her prayers would be heard. His words brought her a deep comfort and a feeling of serenity.

She turned her head away for a moment, and when she turned back, he had disappeared. She looked around the gym, but there was no sign of him anywhere. This man, who had appeared out of the blue, just as mysteriously disappeared.

Rosalie knew that she had experienced the presence of an angel. His energy and words left her feeling calm and peaceful. His love brought with it the gift of healing.

We are not alone. When you are in pain, ask for help. It will be given.

LouLou's Angel

*Who you are is eternal; it never
has and never will change.*

Elisabeth Kubler-Ross, M.D.
Life Lessons

L ouLou, a petite and resilient Frenchwoman, suf-
fers from tachycardia, a medical condition in
which the heart beats rapidly, more than one hundred
beats per minute with at least three irregular beats in a
row. An extremely serious condition, it can develop following a heart attack or in patients with heart failure.
Symptoms include heart palpitations, chest discomfort,
dizziness, shortness of breath, and fainting. Treatment
includes heart medications, but episodes often require
CPR or electrical defibrillation.

When she was diagnosed with tachycardia, LouLou
made significant changes in her lifestyle. She gave up
teaching ballet and playing tennis. She learned to live

with episodes of irregular heart rhythms, but overall, was able to enjoy a relatively good quality of life.

One particular episode LouLou will never forget. She was in bed, not feeling well when she recognized the familiar symptoms. They erupted so quickly that she was unable to move.

LouLou was frightened and called for help. She knew her daughter was home, but when she didn't answer, LouLou felt powerless and became extremely frightened. Only later did she learn that her daughter was in the shower. LouLou struggled to reach the phone by her bed, and although barely able to speak, she managed to dial 911.

When the police and emergency personnel arrived, they broke down the door to her home. As they placed LouLou in the ambulance, she recalled feeling as though she was floating. LouLou had some awareness of what was happening, but remembered little else until she was in the Emergency Room and a team of doctors was shocking her with a defibrillator.

As she was lying on the gurney, she recalled floating high above her body, which was down and to the left. As she floated, she was surrounded by light, but oddly her body, lying on the table below, seemed shrouded in darkness. "There was a body, and it was me," she said. "I was dying. I saw the doctors around me trying to revive me." She continued, "They tried three times. They were using the defibrillator, but nothing happened after the first shock."

"I felt strange. Is this dying?" she wondered. "Oh, I'm dying, and it doesn't hurt!" This surprised her.

Suddenly, LouLou saw her father. He had died fifteen years earlier in her native home, France. She had loved him dearly and missed him. Seeing him was an extraordinary gift.

As the doctors administered, unsuccessfully, a second shock, she heard her father urging her, "Go back, go, go, go!" With his words, she felt him pushing her back into her body, just as the doctors were shocking her for the third and final time.

LouLou heard the doctors shout, "We did it!" and smiling, she said to herself, "No, you didn't do this, my dad did!

Although the Near Death Experience, or NDE, was not frightening for LouLou, the aftermath was traumatizing. It was profoundly distressing to look back and realize that she actually had died, left her body, seen her father, and returned to her body. She did not want to be labeled "crazy, and there was no one with whom she felt safe enough to discuss it. "You have to experience it to understand how it affects you, how it impacts your life."

Years later, LouLou's nephew suffered a severe asthma attack and experienced a similar NDE. He, too, left his body and floated above, looking down as the doctors tried to save him. In his case, his beloved grandmother appeared, urging him to go back into his body. Only after hearing his story, did LouLou feel free to tell her story.

For LouLou, it was a gift to be able to share her thoughts and feelings with her nephew. "Dying is like going from one room to another. It is like going through an invisible door. If it is that easy," she asked, "then why are we all so afraid?"

NDE's are spiritually transformative experiences. They are life-changing events that open up profound possibilities regarding life, dying, the nature of existence, and the nature of a force often referred to as God, Creator, Spirit, or Source.

Those who have experienced NDE's are fortunate to have a knowledge that allows them to live more freely and peacefully. Knowing that there is no suffering as we transition from one energetic state to another brings great comfort. And knowing that our loved ones are with us as we transition helps us in journeying through our grief.

Cascading Light

*Angels represent God's personal
care for each one of us.*

Father Andrew Greeley

On a cold, December morning Sharon sat in my
office glowing with a soft, shimmering light that
emanated from her core. I felt a genuine sense of joy as
I listened to her story (see page 132).

Her mom, during her college years, had joined a
sorority. It was in the 1950s and a time when most
people smoked. Sharon's mom, wanting to feel a part
of her friends' group, also began smoking, and at the
age of sixty-two, was diagnosed with lung cancer.

During her life, she experienced a number of personal disappointments, and although she was very close
to all four of her daughters, she also was not someone
who liked to share her feelings about the difficulties she

had faced. Even when she was diagnosed with cancer and undergoing surgery, chemotherapy, and radiation, she chose not to discuss it.

Sharon and her sisters longed for a chance to talk and reminisce with their mother about their childhood and what they had overcome together, but they respected their mother's privacy. As the weeks and months passed, however, Sharon and her sisters noticed their mother's uncertainty and fear. Sharon said, "A particularly heart-wrenching experience for me was not being able to speak to her about her thoughts and her impending transition into spirit."

She went on, "Because conversations about her relationship with God and the role He was playing in her cancer journey and her life were not taking place, I found I had a greater need to communicate with Him on a regular basis. I am a strong believer in power of prayer and positive thinking. As the days turned into weeks, and my mom's body was not responding to the protocol of treatment, I prayed for God to give her strength, courage, comfort, and most of all, hope."

Sharon believed that whether her mom's path led to continued life on earth or eternal life in spirit, that God's love and grace would sustain them both. She wanted her mom "to have peace in the remaining days of her life."

One night, after going to bed and falling asleep quickly, Sharon felt "gentle nudges on my shoulder that awakened me." She said, "I remember, sleepily, opening my eyes and looking over at my husband, thinking he was the one who had wakened me. But he was sleeping soundly."

"When I turned my head back, I saw a stunning sight outside the French doors of our bedroom. It looked like a waterfall of brilliant, white light streaming down like fireworks on the Fourth of July—an enormous sparkler with unending streams of light cascading down to the ground. The beauty and warmth of the light captivated me. I couldn't take my eyes off of it."

"I felt the presence of something indescribable, a love that filled my soul. I was told by God in a soothing, tranquil manner, 'I am here; I have always been here, and I have never left you. Your prayers have been heard. Take comfort in knowing that there are angels around you and your family. You are loved more than you know. I am here, and everything will be fine. Your faith and continued prayer will sustain you. I am here.'"

Sharon smiled as she wept, realizing she was in the midst of a visit from the Divine. She turned to wake her husband, but God gently told her, "No, this is only for you. Do not wake him."

Sharon turned her gaze back to the waterfall of cascading, shimmering light. She said, "I felt wrapped in a cocoon of love." Her eyelids became heavy, and she was told, "You can lie down and go back to sleep now. I am here." Sharon turned on her side and closed her eyes. Just before she fell asleep, she looked one last time through the French doors, but the cascading, white, shimmering light had disappeared. She slipped into a peaceful sleep.

"Throughout the remainder of my mom's illness

and her eventual transition into spirit, I felt God's presence with every fiber of my being. The visit I received that night embraced and held me in a state of calm, peacefulness, and hope. I feel humbled and grateful for God's presence in my life."

Sharon's prayers were answered, and when her mother eventually died, her daughters at her side, they were comforted by their mutual love for and trust in one another. Sharon feels a profound appreciation for the Universe's gifts. In God sharing His love with her, Sharon learned that "It is abundantly clear that sharing our love with others throughout our lives is the salient purpose of life; in doing so, we honor God."

Sharon's experience of the cascading, white, shimmering light is similar to the light that Dr. Frank Oski, a renowned pediatric professor at Johns Hopkins University, discovered in his bedroom late one night. His story has been published in a well known pediatric journal.

As a medical student, he had been caring for a young child, but in spite of his efforts, the child had died. That night, feeling helpless, Dr. Oski, like Sharon, prayed to God, asking why young patients sometimes die. Not long after falling asleep, he was awakened by an immense, bright light that filled the room. As he opened his eyes, he was stunned to see before him an angelic being who told him in a hushed voice that some children come into this world to teach us all how to love; those with disabilities teach us how to love one who is imperfect. The angel acknowledged that some of his patients would die, but reassured him that he needed to continue with his work, that he came into this life to help children heal.

When I first heard Dr. Oski's story, I was deeply touched and remembered it upon hearing Sharon's story of her own meeting with an angelic light. For both, the Light reassured them that they were on the right path and being watched over and protected.

9

Answered Prayers

*P*rayer, meditation, finding silence; these are all ways that people tap into the energy that connects them to the universe. Being open to such possibilities does not minimize what medicine can do; It makes the potential endless.

WILLIAM E. HABLITZEL, M.D.,
Dying Was the Best Thing That Ever Happened to Me

The Cameo

It is impossible to have a prayer without power.
It is impossible to have a thought that
is a secret, for all energy is heard.
When you pray, you draw to you and
invoke grace. Grace . . . is Divinity.

Gary Zukav, Ph. D.

On a warm, cloudy but beautiful, fall Saturday in
October, my husband and I sat in a small room
of a cameo factory in Naples, Italy with the owners,
two stately gentlemen, who also were brothers. We
were choosing cameos to buy for two special souls in
our lives. One was for a dear friend who loves cameos,
the other for Samantha.

What I did not know until we gave Samantha the
cameo a few weeks later was that she had always longed
for a cameo. Many years before, she and her family were
traveling from Russia and had stopped in Italy to wait
for permission to enter the Unites States. One day she
accompanied her mother to a store that sold cameos.
One cameo in particular caught her eye. She quickly fell

in love with the portrait of the woman that had been so exquisitely carved out of a sea shell. The cameo cost twenty-five dollars, and since her mom was buying jewelry for herself, Samantha dearly hoped that her mom also would buy this one special cameo for Samantha. But her mom adamantly refused. Sam was heartbroken.

Sam longed for this piece of jewelry for decades and was visibly surprised when she opened our gift. She stared at the face on the cameo in disbelief and gratitude.

"Susan," she said, "This is so extraordinary of you!" She told us how the face on the cameo was so like the one she had fallen in love with many years before in Italy. She confided that she had never forgotten the face and had always hoped someday to have a cameo similar to it. As she gazed at the cameo, she shared with me that the cameo's portrait resembled her daughter.

I was touched by her response and moved by her story. What impressed me most was that for all these years she had held onto her memory of the cameo, hoping to have one for herself.

Because of this, it eventually came to her. Samantha did not live her life attached to her desire for the cameo, but she held on to her dream and desire, surrendered to it, and in time, it came to her.

Her story reminds us all to hold on to our dreams and desires, but do not be attached to them. Know what you want, ask for it, and release it. Live your life from a place of joy, peace, and passion; by being in a place of higher energy, you will attract to yourself those dreams and desires you hoped for.

Mary Ellen's Prayer

Through prayer, love is received, and
through miracles, love is expressed.

A Course in Miracles

Mary Ellen survived the breakup of her marriage of eighteen years in 1996 and the loss of her mother in late January, 2000.

Following her divorce, as a single working mom with three children, ages eleven to seventeen, she began teaching, as non-contracted faculty, gifted second graders in the Council Rock School District in Bucks County, Pennsylvania.

In October, a few months before her mother's death, Mary Ellen noticed a pain in her back. She started to lose weight and developed a rash on her body. One doctor diagnosed shingles, another anxiety; a third concluded she was suffering from muscular problems.

All wanted to prescribe medication, although nothing conclusive was indicated by any of the tests that had been ordered. By February the pain in her back worsened. She called a friend, a doctor, who told her to go to the emergency room where he ordered a cat scan with contrast dye, a test she'd not had previously. The doctor saw "something suspicious" on her lung and asked her to come in for a biopsy.

Divorced and with her mother gone, Mary Ellen was very much alone. She had to drive herself to the hospital the day of the procedure. She had no loved ones waiting for her in the waiting room, as the technicians told her to lie still, injecting the needle into the tumor to extract cells.

The day after her biopsy, she received a call from the doctor telling her she had Non- Hodgkin's Lymphoma. She was stunned but grateful to him for the support and hope he offered as he told her, "Don't worry, Mary Ellen. This is a treatable form of the disease."

She sought a second opinion at another major medical center where the original findings were confirmed, but the "Stage 1V B Cell Non Hodgkin's Lymphoma, with only a 50% chance of survival," seemed a far less hopeful diagnosis.

Mary Ellen's strength and intuitiveness, her take-charge style, and her attitude led her to choose a doctor and a facility that provided her with hope. She knew that, for her body to heal, she needed affirmative words and actions.

Mary Ellen's conviction that she would beat her disease allowed her to go into treatments assured that she would do what she needed to do. Her protocol required that she receive very powerful and aggressive chemotherapy every three weeks. Because she did not want to risk losing her teaching position, she scheduled her treatments for Friday afternoons, allowing herself the weekend to recover before returning to work on Monday mornings. Unfortunately, the impact of the treatments took a progressively greater toll on her than she had anticipated, and by the fourth treatment, it was necessary for her to take off Fridays and Mondays. Mary Ellen gave herself permission to do this by declining payment for those missed days.

The treatments caused her to lose significant strength in her legs and body; it became difficult for her to carry even her book bag. But her friends helped with this, and she received other extraordinary, heartfelt, unexpected gifts of love from members of the community. Her neighbors formed a group called *Angels for Mary*. They drove her to work, helped her with her lesson plans, prayed for her. Every night of the week, a homemade dinner for her and her children was delivered to her home by these angels.

Throughout her treatments, Mary Ellen was able to maintain her sense of humor, joking that having home-cooked meals and not having to blow-dry her hair were reasons to be happy. She experienced the loss of her hair, eyebrows, and eyelashes by her third chemo treatment. It was not easy, but Mary Ellen accepted this as part of the process. She wore her wig to work, but at the end of the day, as soon as she got into her car to drive home, she took off her wig and put on her favorite baseball cap.

She also was very grateful for her teaching; focusing on her students and their needs helped her through her treatments by balancing her life with a concern for others and providing her with something else to think about besides cancer.

Her friends gave her a statue of the Virgin Mary. Mary Ellen, who is Catholic, thought it would be good to offer a novena and wrote a letter to the Virgin Mary. In writing her letter, she felt as though she was speaking directly to Mary, and she believed that she was being heard. When she prayed to Mary, she asked to receive something, a rose or a sign from either Mary or Saint Theresa of the Little Flower that promised she would experience healing.

A few days later, while driving home from school, a cardinal flew directly in front of her car, and just missed being hit. The following day she experienced another cardinal flying right in front of the car, and later, she saw a cardinal on her deck. Mary believed that this sudden appearance of red cardinals was the Virgin Mary's sign that she was going to be OK. She felt profoundly grateful, and even now when a cardinal comes into her path, Mary Ellen prays and gives thanks. Cardinals have become representative of something extraordinary, even sacred, in her life.

Mary believes that her prayers were heard and answered. By the time she received her fourth treatment, the cancer was in remission. The original tumor, the size of a tennis ball and located between her lung and the chest wall in her back, shrank and disappeared. More good news followed the same day she learned she was in remission; she received a phone call from her school principal informing her that she was being offered a full time teaching contact with the Council Rock School District. Mary Ellen felt assured that she would be able to finish her treatments and rest over the summer before returning, replenished, to school in the fall.

The treatments, however did take a toll. Although the pain in her back lessened, she experienced terrible pain in the bones of her hips, thighs, and legs, and when at home, often needed to slide up and down the stairs on her bottom. She became increasingly frail.

However, Mary Ellen is an extremely resilient, wise, and strong woman. She recently reached her five year anniversary mark and celebrated by treating herself to a brand new convertible—cardinal red, of course! She chooses to visualize herself as well and happy and continues to give thanks to Saint Teresa and the Virgin Mary for watching over her.

Letter to the Virgin Mary

Dear Mary,

How appropriate it is for me to pray to you in the year of the third millennium for the opportunity to watch my three children grow up. Just like you, I am a single mother, and my children don't have any close family other than me. I know that you are their family, too, but children need a mother's warm shoulder to lean on, just as I need your guidance.

Please don't let my prayers go unanswered. Please allow me to watch my children grow up, and as the Irish blessing goes, see their children's children.

I pray daily for you to lead me on the right track toward healing. I pray to be cured of Non-Hodgkin's Lymphoma, and I pray for my tumor not to invade my lungs. I pray to you that I may live a little longer, so that I can have the opportunity to make a difference in this world. This is not only for my own children, but for all those children whom I teach.

I am not afraid to die and meet God. I just would like to stay with my family on Earth a little longer. They need me, too.

Everything I have been reading repeats that you do not let any prayers go unanswered.

Please hear mine.

Mary Ellen

Answered Prayers

Prayer is the medium of miracles.
It is a means of communication of
the created with the Creator.

A Course in Miracles

We are here to live in peace, not to suffer. Always we are in the loving care of energetic forces that wish to ease our pain, to make our lives a bit easier. Hope comes to us in knowing that we can ask for help, and when we ask for help, we will receive it. Knowing that help is always available enables us to live more fully, more confidently, more lovingly.

Asking for help is a form of prayer. Something as simple as "Please help me." is a prayer. We do not need to be fancy but only to speak from our hearts, because this is where truth lives.

Several years ago, I was on my computer struggling with a chapter in my first book. It was a rainy, spring day, and I was rushing to meet a deadline when everything just stopped working. I was distressed and concerned about meeting my responsibilities.

I remember praying, with all my heart, asking for God and my angels to please find a way to help me. I had no idea how I was going to get someone with computer experience to come to my home on such little notice. But I sat at my desk, prayed for help, then went to the phonebook and dialed a computer service company. No one picked up so I left a message, and much to my amazement, within an hour, I received a call telling me that someone would be coming out shortly to help me.

When the gentleman arrived, he got right down to the work of fixing my computer. As he finished up, he said to me, "You know, I was really busy today, and I normally don't come out on this kind of job. But when I heard your voice, I felt that maybe I could help you and decided to come myself." It was at that moment that I knew my prayers had been heard, and a mini-miracle had occurred. I felt such a sense of loving gratitude to my angels for having heard me.

Just recently I experienced another gift from my angels. During a very intense summer thunderstorm, a large tree branch came crashing down on our porch roof. When I looked at the large hole, I knew that I needed help fast. Remnants of a hurricane were heading up the coast, and the weatherman was predicting torrential rains for the next several days. I was extremely worried, knowing that water could easily flood our garden room and basement.

Again I prayed, asking for help finding someone who could come and repair the hole in the roof until we could have the entire roof replaced. I knew this would be difficult, especially because it was a Friday. When I finished expressing my gratitude for my blessings and asking for help, I then went downstairs, opened the phonebook, called a familiar name, and left my plea for help. Again, much to my delight, I received a call from the owner of the business saying that he would be at my home within the hour.

Well, at 10:30 a.m., a tall, bearded, kindly man came to my door. I showed him the hole in the roof, and he went to work covering the hole so that there could be no water leakage. Forty-five minutes later, and sweating profusely, he came to tell me that the hole was temporarily repaired.

While I was writing out my check to him, he said something familiar. He said, "You know, I do not work on Fridays, and I was just going out the door when the phone rang. I was not even going to answer it. In fact, this is a job I usually give my crew to do. But, something compelled me to pick up the phone . . . and here I am."

How grateful I was to him and to my angels for hearing my prayer.

My prayers also have included that my book, *Touched by the Extraordinary*, finds its way to those who truly are in need of comfort, hope, and healing.

Shortly after its publication, I attended a psychology seminar and was blessed to meet another psychologist, Bonnie Frank Carter. Because of traffic we both arrived late and ended up seated near one another. At lunch she asked to buy a copy of my book.

In the months that followed, she not only read my book but purchased seventy copies to give to her friends and family in celebration of her sixtieth birthday.

Bonnie wrote the following inscription in the gift books:

As Michelangelo said, 'I am still learning.' And with the recent unexpected occurrences in my life, along with turning sixty in July 2008, there always seems to be more to learn. Significant among my many lessons is the fundamental role of faith in everyone's life. Either you have it, or you are still looking for it.

Please accept this gift of Touched by the Extraordinary *as a thank-you for maintaining your faith in me, even as I continue learning. It is my hope that Susan Apollon's words will provide replenishment and encouragement as you continue your own personal journey, and serve as a reminder that you are an extraordinary person."*

Bonnie also wrote a note to me that I wish to share with you.

The thank-you responses already coming in make it clear that I was correct in wanting to spread the valuable wisdom and experiences contained in your marvelous book. . . .

I first learned about you and your book when The Philadelphia Inquirer ran an interview. I was intrigued, but it somehow took awhile longer before I purchased it and began to read.

One of my favorite expressions is that 'Steam engines come at steam engine time,' supposedly referring to an Egyptologist's response when heckled during a lecture: if the Egyptians were so great, why didn't they invent the steam engine? Well, your book found its way to me just at its right time. I was just beginning to recognize the true enormousness of the Universe and the true range of our souls' iterations.

Somehow, after a lifetime of hard-science, limited vision, and fairly entrenched atheism, I began to 'see' the legitimate presence of meaningful co-occurrences.

You do not travel this road alone. When you begin to open your heart to the possibility of this and to ask those you do not see for assistance, you will be pleasantly surprised and supported in all you do. This started with the presence of pelicans and Canadian geese after my father's death (I am sure he had a lot to do with my changed vision, as well as other changes in my life.) and has continued in many other arenas with the introduction into my life of a young woman who 'sees' so much more than I, and, yet, we both continue learning.

It truly was an extraordinary occurrence when I attended a seminar last winter and discovered that I was seated immediately in front of you! Having you join me for lunch that day also was a gift. Your understanding and deeply respectful encouragement for further learning and experience remain on-going resources.

How blessed I was to receive Bonnie's note, to know that the messages of hope and healing in *Touched by the Extraordinary* are finding their way into the world.

Conclusion

Love is always present in my life, in all our
wonderful experiences—and even in our tragedies.
Love is what gives our days their meaning;
it is what we are truly made of.
Whatever we call it—love, God, soul—love is
alive and tangible, living within all of us.
It is ours for the taking.

David Kessler, *Life Lessons*

By now, you have a sense of the many ways in which your journey through life—through love, loss, and hope—contributes to your growth, helping you to become more enlightened and even transformed. Perhaps you also are questioning what is real and what is not.

This is how it goes. Your soul arrives in a physical body, aware that your journey is filled with countless and surprising opportunities—people, places, experiences—that will help you on your path; how you choose to respond to these ever-changing opportunities affects the person you are at this very minute, reading this.

Here is the interesting thing. Whomever you believe yourself to be, right now, is not who you are. You are so much more. Even as you look at these words, believing they are real, they, too, are not what they seem. All of this is an illusion, a mysterious orbit you created because, at this moment in time, it is what you need or will need in your future.

If you are open to the possibilities inherent in the stories I've offered, you have the ability to more fully realize your potential; you also are able to communicate intuitively, at a higher level, and with energy that is not attached to a body. The stories are a testament to the innate power in all of us. With this awareness of power, comes hope.

When we learn to attribute meaning to the events in our lives, we connect with our Higher Purpose, Higher Wisdom, or Source; we become Master of the Self. A gradual process, this often is tied to loss and to love.

The more frequently we confront the painful separation of someone or something we have loved, the more frequently we tap into a consciousness of connection, becoming more attuned to our inherent wisdom. Genuine amazement and respect for what has occurred nurtures an increased awareness of our powers, and we are in awe!

In writing *Touched by the Extraordinary*, I learned that not only are we all touched by extraordinary events, but more importantly, we, ourselves, are truly extraordinary. Knowing this allows us to live in a place in which love is the dominant energy, the force that both heals and connects us. Knowing this also nurtures a sense of hope.

When we understand the illusory nature of life and the profound power of eternal love, which enables us to create miracles and experience the presence of our deceased loved ones, we find ourselves living with joy, hope, and peace.

Filling ourselves and living with the energy of love feels wonderful. And because this energy resonates at a high vibrational level, it also attracts into our lives other high, vibrational experiences, many of which feel quite miraculous.

In *A Course in Miracles,* Dr. Helen Shucman, dictating the inner voice of a non-denominational divine source, maintains that love is what engenders miracles, and that miracles are happening all the time! Whether illusions, miracles, or extraordinary happenings, these experiences have the power to balance and complete us, to comfort and to heal.

The power of love is the key to miracles, to having hope, and to prayer.

My assistant, CoraLyn, an authentic, beautiful soul, lives in Phoenix, and shared a story that validates not only the power of prayer, but also that our loved ones continue to care lovingly for us, even when they are in a non-physical state.

According to Cora, several years ago, she was sick with the flu. Fortunately, it was a Saturday, and her friend, Nancy, stopped by with groceries. While Nancy was there, Cora excused herself to go to the bathroom, although when she was in the bathroom, she found that she was unable to urinate. When she returned to the living room, Nancy was "white as a sheet." She told Cora that Cora's mom, Sunny, had just been there. Cora adored her mom, who had died many years before.

Stunned, Cora asked her friend, "What was she wearing?" Nancy replied, "An off the shoulder number." Cora smiled, knowing this was in keeping with her mom's style. Cora also noticed the scent of Chanel No. 5, her mom's favorite perfume, which lingered in the living room throughout the weekend. Though comforted, Cora was too ill to realize that her mother was warning her to get to the hospital.

By Monday morning, Cora felt extremely weak. She called her friend, Chris, asking to be taken to St. Joseph's Hospital. When she told the Emergency Room staff that she had not been able to urinate since Saturday, they immediately admitted her and ordered several tests. The staff, noting that Cora was unable to turn over or to sit up, administered diuretic and radioactive isotopes. They also discovered that she was in kidney and liver failure. They scheduled emergency surgery to remove her gallbladder and learned that it was the ibuprofen she had been directed to take by her physician that had caused the kidney and liver failure.

Regaining consciousness after the surgery, Cora found she was on a ventilator. She could hear soft, soothing music. She recently had been reading Shirley MacLaine's book, *Going Within,* in which MacLaine discusses chakras. Cora said, "I recall being in my bed in Intensive Care, not feeling well, and visualizing the clearing of my chakras. I remembered, fortunately, the colors red, orange, and yellow, which, luckily, cover the liver and kidney areas."

When the ventilator was removed, Cora needed dialysis for three days. This caused her to feel exceptionally weak, but while she was lying there, she continued to visualize clearing her chakras while reciting the Lord's Prayer. The nuns asked her if they could do anything for her, and at her request, promised her that they would pray for her recovery.

After the first day, Cora noticed miraculous changes taking place. "Everything started working that day—everything!" Her doctors and nurses monitored her closely for three weeks until she finally healed and was well enough to leave.

She told me, "I know that my mother, Sunny, closely watches over me from the other side, and I am not alone. I am also so grateful to her for her teaching me to be open to everything, including those things people tend to consider 'out of the ordinary—or extraordinary.'"

Love is the force behind prayer, the force behind hope and miracles.

Life brings us many challenges, but when we are facing loss and trauma, our choices determine not only our quality of life, but also our joy. Choose to be open, to love with your heart, and to listen to the wisdom of your intuitive self—that part connected with and aware of being in the Oneness. By embracing this, you will be able to create the illusions you wish to have in your life.

A final story I would like to share took place within the past two months of my life and speaks to the awareness of our interconnectedness to each other and to the Oneness. Incorporating the healing elements of love, loss, and hope, the story validates the belief that, in choosing love, we learn we are not alone, that loss is an illusion, and that hope is the gift that accompanies the choices we make in desiring a life of bliss and peace.

May you know always that you are never alone, that life and love are eternal, and that you are extraordinary.

The Loving Gift of the Spirit Rose

She was the angel the Universe sent to me, the guide I needed to help me manifest my dream of writing a book that would help so many to heal. She was Bev—wife, mother, poet—my dear, wise friend, always laughing, and with a love for life. She reminded me of a leprechaun or an angel, weaving the magic of her poetic words and sensibility into the language of my book.

While editing the stories for *Touched by the Extraordinary*, Bev acknowledged that she had her favorites. Many reminded her of the special moments in her own life, especially those that evoked memories of her son, David, who died at twenty-seven. Because of her own painful loss, Bev was able to bring to *Touched by the Extraordinary*, the feelings experienced by every mother who has lost a child.

One story that fascinated Bev was about cameos, for which I have a deep fondness. In the story, a friend of mine, while cooking Sunday dinner for her family, experienced a visit from my mother, who had died several years before. My mom wanted to share with my friend a new perspective on the meaning of the cameos my husband had given to me over many years.

Bev also was fascinated with cameos, and one lovely spring day, in 1999, while we were having lunch at the Yardley Inn, along the Delaware River, Bev surprised me with a very special gift. She handed me a beautifully wrapped box, and as I unfolded the delicate, white, tissue paper, I was delighted to find the most exquisitely carved, small, oval cameo. On the face of the cameo was a perfectly carved rose. It just touched my heart! Bev, who knew how much I loved cameos, had wanted me to have this gift of a rose cameo so that I would have something precious from her. I certainly would treasure her gift for the rest of my life.

Little did I know how meaningful her gift would become. In December 2008, Bev died. Those of us who loved her felt an enormous loss and sadness.

In August 2009, I was honored to be asked by Bev's daughter, Val, to read one of Bev's poems at her memorial service. The service was to be held at Bucks County Community College in Newtown, Pennsylvania, where Bev had taught writing and literature and often participated in poetry workshops.

Val sent a copy of the poem she wanted me to read; imagine my astonishment when I saw that the poem was titled, "The Rose."

The evening of the memorial service, Bev's family, friends, and colleagues gathered in the Orangery. Those reading Bev's poems sat in a large semi-circle behind which was a courtyard and gardens. Around the room were several tables covered with Bev's favorite cloths and filled with family photographs, shells, books of poetry, and vases brimming with homegrown, summer flowers brought by her friends. There also were pies and cakes and Bev's favorite—Katherine Hepburn Brownies—baked by her family and friends who were honoring her with their love and presence.

As I sat waiting my turn to read, the thirteenth of fourteen readers, I could feel the loving energy generated by everyone and everything in the room. Love permeated all of us, and Bev's energy was tangible.

As Val spoke of her mom and what poetry meant to Bev, I could see Bev's profile in her daughter's face. As we listened to the poems being read, Val placed her hand in mine, sharing her and her mom's loving energy with me. It was then that I welled up with tears, and again a few minutes later, as I stood at the podium to speak, sharing with all the synchronicity of being given the beautiful rose cameo and being asked to read Bev's poem, "The Rose."

Bev's family, graciously, has consented to sharing her poem with you.

THE SPIRIT ROSE

The Spirit Rose is given by the departed as a gift
of gratitude for favors bestowed during life.
One morning when you are writing,
your eyes will be drawn to the skylight
above your desk, and you'll think at first
it's a trick of the sun, the extravagant light,
or, if winter, that frost etched a design on the
slanted pane.
But seeing clearly its perfection—
long curving stem, picot-edged leaves,
capped bud—you'll know it's not
a natural occurrence, and trace the lines
with your fingertips, trying to erase them,
all your senses alive.
You'll imagine the rose a luminous red, petals
lambent, scent more pungent than perfumed.
Puzzled, you'll reflect on how it came to be,
while I, drifting ever more deeply into
the spirit world, aware that I can't stay
long, will hold on, rebellious, resistant,
insisting on being present to see your
wonder at my gift.

Beverly Foss Stoughton

Appendix

Healing from Grief and Trauma

In the middle of difficulty lies opportunity.

Albert Einstein

Recently, our good friends' son, a young man we watched grow up, died in a freak accident. Another dear friend was hospitalized with septicemia and suddenly fighting for her life. My patients, friends, and family can testify to the quirkiness of life; one minute all is well, and the next, our life is totally upside down. Each time we experience a loss or a trauma, we are reminded that life is a precious and fragile gift. This awareness is the first lesson in learning to deal with loss.

When difficult situations arise, we often fail to realize that we have a choice in how we interpret the meaning of the loss or trauma. During the initial grieving process, we, understandably, feel devastated and alone, but in the months and years that follow, we can slow our healing by continuing to expend negative thoughts and energy.

Why is this? Perhaps, it is the fear that what has happened can happen again. Perhaps, it is because we focus on the experience as a loss, and therefore, spend energy dwelling on the pain of separation from our loved one rather than on something of value in our lives. Our nature is to obsess more about our adversity than about those elements in our lives that bring us joy.

The truth is that the way in which we consider a situation influences powerfully the healing of our body, mind, and spirit.

After years of working with and learning from my patients, I offer the following suggestions to help you in healing from loss and trauma.

1. Give yourself permission to feel your pain.

   Healing from loss and trauma takes time. Grieving is an experience that affects every aspect of your body, mind, and spirit. No matter how you try to avoid it, your Higher Self will demand that you do the work of grief. Trying to escape the pain does not serve you. Healing is expedited when you do the best you can to express it, feel it, and let it go.

2. Be open to changing your perspective.

   Experiencing grief helps us to reestablish priorities in life. What was once highly valued, a fancy car, for instance, or even a job, may have decreased importance.

3. Recognize the importance of love.

We learn, through pain and suffering, that the only thing that truly matters is the people you love. My husband taught me this before we were married. Walking along a boat dock, I was carrying his watch and rings when they suddenly slipped from my hands and fell between the cracks into the water. I was in tears and feeling great guilt, but I will always remember his words: "Don't worry, Susan. The only thing that matters is you. I can replace the jewelry; I can't replace you." His love touched me and soothed my pain of disappointing him!

4. Discover how strong you really are.

You might be forced suddenly into roles that your ill or deceased loved one once held. Finding or holding down a full-time job, paying bills, maintaining a home, a car, and creating a new social life can be difficult, but you will discover that you now are taking responsibility for areas of your life that you previously felt unable to handle.

5. You are more powerful, more capable, and more resilient than you realize.

This new awareness may enhance your self-esteem, self-confidence, and a belief in yourself. Surviving a profound loss will validate your sense of internal strength and resiliency. Ironically, these gifts are given to you at a time when you feel powerless, frightened, and worried about surviving.

6. What is this experience teaching me? What is the lesson I need to learn here?

   Asking these questions rather than "Why did this happen?" will help to generate an enhanced ability to cope with your loss. Asking "What is the lesson?" will help you to move away from the feeling that you are a victim and towards the realization that you are a resourceful person with a sense of purpose.

7. Consider your loss or trauma as an opportunity to learn valuable life lessons: patience, courage, compassion, and forgiveness.

   A stronger sense of self will lead to a stronger connection with your own Higher Power or God. This, in turn, will lead to a change in perspective about the meaning of your loss. As your perspective broadens, the possibilities about life and its purpose also will deepen. This growth in perspective comforts and heals the pain of your broken heart.

8. Balance your body, mind, and spirit with lighter energy.

   The pain of a loss or trauma is locked into your cells and can weaken your immune system. Healing mentally and spiritually requires that you heal physically. Even if you do not feel like laughing, spend time with friends, watch a comedy on TV, or enjoy a dinner out. Balancing your pain with a lighter energy will protect your body from the aftermath of trauma.

9. Allow yourself to feel the outpouring of love.

When we are grieving, we often find that our family and friends shower us with compassion, kindness, and prayers. Allowing yourself to be touched by their love is transformative. Often, those grieving will themselves become more caring and compassionate. Stepping out of your own pain to help another in distress will heal not only you, but help to heal the other. Becoming aware of the power of your own love also will help you to become more appreciative of your blessings. Take time to express your heartfelt thanks. This, too, expedites your healing process.

10. Stay rooted in the present.

This is difficult, but it is essential. If you are plagued by pain, feelings of guilt, and responsibility, acknowledge the pain and feel it, but come back to the present moment. Meditation, or even taking several deep breaths while focusing on the breath, will bring a sense of calmness and peace. Forgive yourself and release the past.

11. You are shifting to a higher level of consciousness.

In working through the challenges of a major loss we are blessed to have a heightened awareness of how precious life is. Observe carefully your own thoughts and the meaning of your loss in relationship to your physical, emotional, and spiritual healing. An increased spirituality heals the body, mind, and spirit.

12. Be conscious of how you are feeling and how you speak of your experience.

Treat yourself and speak of your experience with love, kindness, and compassion as you would a parent caring for and soothing a hurt child.

About the Author

Susan Apollon is an intuitive psychologist, psychotherapist, and healer. For more than two decades, she has specialized in treating children and adults who are traumatized, grieving, ill with chronic or life-threatening diseases, and/or dying. As a master of several healing and energy modalities, a researcher of mind, consciousness, energy, and metaphysics, a student and teacher of intuition, and a survivor of her own challenge with breast cancer, her intention is to bring wisdom, compassion, and peace to those with whom she works.

An award-winning author, Susan wrote and recorded the book and an eleven-audio CD package, *Touched by the Extraordinary: An Intuitive Psychologist Shares Insights, Lessons, and True Stories of Spirit and Love to Transform and Heal the Soul*. She also has created CDs and DVDs of her meditations and presentations, in order to assist those desiring relaxation and healing.

She is a contributing author, along with Mark Victor Hansen and Les Brown, to *101 Great Ways to Improve Your Life*. Additionally, Susan is the co-author of the book, audio book, and online course, *Intuition is Easy and Fun*, which she created with Yanni Maniates, a renowned teacher of intuition and meditation.

Her articles have appeared in newspapers and magazines across the country as well as in celebrated internet journals and websites. Susan also is a frequent guest on national radio and television shows. Susan and Yanni have been honored by an invitation to teach in 2009 at the winter campus of the Omega Institute of Holistic Studies in Costa Rica.

Susan believes in the wisdom and capability of each human being to achieve self-mastery. She speaks passionately, often as a keynote speaker, to hospital staffs and patients, nursing and medical students, organizations and groups about the ability to live a full, satisfying life, healing from illness and grief, and creating happiness and miracles. Her workshops and seminars provide a blend of contagious enthusiasm with established methods and interventions for healing, empowerment, and creating a healthy and joyful life.

Susan's love of medicine and healing has its roots in her lineage; she comes from a family of physicians. She has been married for more than forty years to her husband and soul mate, Warren, an orthodontist, and she is the proud mom of Rebecca, an emergency medicine physician, and David, a management consultant. She also is a passionate advocate for animals and the environment.

For more information, please visit
www.TouchedByTheExtraordinary.com
www.LoveToFeelGoodBlog.com
www.IntuitionIsEasyAndFun.com

e-mail: susan@mattersofthesoul.com
Phone: 215-321-0632

With Gratitude and How to Contact the Author

Susan is extremely grateful for you selecting *Healing Stories of Love, Loss and Hope* for yourself or a loved one. She wrote this book for all of us who have experienced a loss and are in need of healing and the restoration of balance, wholeness and well-being.

. . . .

If you have experienced an extraordinary, unique and inspirational story of love, loss and hope that you would like to share with Susan . . .
Or
If you would like to have Susan speak to your organization or at an upcoming event,
Please contact her at:
Matters of the Soul, LLC
PO Box 403, Yardley, PA 19067
PHONE: 215-321-0632 or 215-493-8434
FAX: 215-321-3830
E-MAIL: susan@mattersofthesoul.com

. . . .

Susan would also love to have you join her on
Facebook in one or more of her groups:
Touched by the Extraordinary
HOPE, TRUST & MIRACLES in the Midst of Challenge
INTUITION: The Voice of Wisdom & Truth

Order Form

ONLINE ORDERS   www.TouchedByTheExtraordinary.com

TELEPHONE ORDERS Call 1-888-768-8353 (credit cards)

FAX ORDERS   215-321-3830

POSTAL ORDERS   Matters of the Soul, LLC

                  PO Box 403, Yardley, PA 19067

QUESTIONS   215-321-0632 or susan@mattersofthesoul.com

TOUCHED BY THE EXTRAORDINARY PRODUCTS		PRICE	QTY	SUBTOTAL
Book Two: Healing Stories of Love, Loss and Hope	HARDCOVER	$24.95	_____	_____
Audio Book (read by the author)	4 CDS	$34.95	_____	_____
	MP3s	$17.95	_____	_____
Book One & Book Two Set	COMBO	$35.00	_____	_____
Touched by the Extraordinary	SOFTCOVER	$19.95		_____
Audio Book	11 CDS	$79.95	_____	_____
	MP3s	$29.95	_____	_____
*SALES TAX: Pennsylvania addresses add 6%				_____
**US SHIPPING: $4.50 for first product and $1.00 for each additional				_____
**PRIORITY MAIL: $7.95				
please call or e-mail for international shipping rates				
TOTAL				_____

SOLD TO

Name: _____

Address: _____

City, State Zip: _____

Telephone: _____

E-mail: _____

SEND TO

Name: _____

Address: _____

City, State Zip: _____

PAYMENT

❑ Check enclosed   ❑ VISA   ❑ Master Card

Card Number _____

Exp. Date _____   Security Code _____